FROM SEA TO SEA

LETTERS OF TRAVEL

AMERICAN NOTES

From Sea to Sea

Letters of Travel
American Notes

By
Rudyard Kipling

GARDEN CITY   NEW YORK
DOUBLEDAY, DORAN & COMPANY, INC.
1928

FROM SEA TO SEA

MARCH–SEPTEMBER, 1889

No. I

OF FREEDOM AND THE NECESSITY OF USING HER. THE
MOTIVE AND THE SCHEME THAT WILL COME TO NOTHING.
A DISQUISITION UPON THE OTHERNESS OF THINGS AND
THE TORMENTS OF THE DAMNED.

> When all the world is young, lad,
>   And all the trees are green,
> And every goose a swan, lad,
>   And every lass a queen, —
> Then hey for boot and horse, lad,
>   And o'er the world away —
> Young blood must have its course, lad,
>   And every dog its day.

AFTER seven years it pleased Necessity, whom we all
serve, to turn to me and say: "Now you need do Nothing
Whatever. You are free to enjoy yourself. I will take
the yoke of bondage from your neck for one year. What
do you choose to do with my gift?" And I considered
the matter in several lights. At first I held notions
of regenerating Society; but it appeared that this
would demand more than a year, and perhaps Society
would not be grateful after all. Then I would fain enter
upon one monumental "bust"; but I reflected that this
at the outside could endure but three months, while the

o   193

headache would last for nine. Then came by the person that I most hate,—a Globe-trotter. He, sitting in my chair, discussed India with the unbridled arrogance of five weeks on a Cook's ticket. He was from England and had dropped his manners in the Suez Canal. "I assure you," said he, "that you who live so close to the actual facts of things cannot form dispassionate judg ments of their merits. You are too near. Now I—" he waved his hand modestly and left me to fill the gaps.

I considered him, from his new helmet to his deck-shoes, and I perceived that he was but an ordinary man. I thought of India, maligned and silent India, given up to the ill-considered wanderings of such as he—of the land whose people are too busy to reply to the libels upon their life and manners. It was my destiny to avenge India upon nothing less than three-quarters of the world. The idea necessitated sacrifices,—painfv' sacrifices,—for I had to become a Globe-trotter, with a helmet and deck-shoes. In the interests of our little world I would endure these things and more. I would deliver "brawling judgments all day long; on all things unashamed." I would go toward the rising sun till I reached the heart of the world and once more smelt London asphalt.

The Indian public never gave me a brief. I took it, appointing myself Commissioner in General for Our Own Sweet Selves. Then all the aspects of life changed, as, they say, the appearance of his room grows strange to a dying man when he sees it upon the last morning, and knows that it will confront him no more. I had wilfully stepped aside from the current of our existence, and had no part in any of Our interests. Up-country the peach was beginning to bud, and men said that by cause of the heavy snows in the Hills the hot weather would be a short one. That was nothing to me. The punkahs and their pullers sat together in the verandah, and the public buildings spawned thermantidotes. The copper-smith sang in the garden and the early wasp hummed low down by the door-handle, and they prophesied of the hot weather to come. These things were no concern of mine. I was dead, and looked upon the old life as a dead man — without interest and without concern.

It was a strange life; I had lived it for seven years or one day, I could not be certain which. All that I knew was that I could watch men going to their offices, while I slept luxuriously ; could go out at any hour of the day and sit up to any hour of the night, secure that each morning would bring no toil. I understood with what emotions the freed convict regards the prison he has quitted — insight which had hitherto been denied me; and I further saw how intense is the selfishness of the irresponsible man. Some said that the coming year would be one of scarcity and distress because unseasonable rains were falling. I was grieved. I feared that the Rains might break the railway line to the sea, and so delay my departure. Again, the season would be a sickly one. I fancied that Necessity might repent of her gift and for mere jest wipe me off the face of the earth ere I had seen anything of what lay upon it. There was trouble on the Afghan frontier; perhaps an army-corps would be mobilised, and perhaps many men would die, leaving folk to mourn for them at the hill-stations. My dread was that a Russian man-of-war might intercept the steamer which carried my precious self between Yokohama and San Francisco. Let **Arma**geddon be postponed, I prayed, for my sake, that my personal enjoyments may not be interfered with. War, famine, and pestilence would be so inconvenient to me. And I abased myself before Necessity, the great Goddess, and said ostentatiously: "It is naught, it is naught, and you needn't look at me when I wander about." Surely we are only virtuous by compulsion of earning our daily bread.

So I looked upon men with new eyes, and pitied them very much indeed. They worked. They had to. I was an aristocrat. I could call upon them at inconvenient hours and ask them why they worked, and whether they did it often. Then they grunted, and the envy in their eyes was a delight to me. I dared not, however, mock them too pointedly, lest Necessity should drag me back by the collar to take my still warm place by their side. When I had disgusted all who knew me, I fled to Calcutta, which, I was pained to see, still persisted in being a city and transacting commerce after I had formally cursed it one year ago. That curse I now repeat, in the hope that the unsavoury capital will collapse. One must begin to smoke at five in the morning — which is neither night nor day — on coming across the Howrah Bridge, for it is better to get a headache from honest nicotine than to be poisoned by evil smells. And a man, who otherwise was a nice man, though he worked with his hands and his head, asked me why the scandal of the Simla Exodus was allowed to continue. To him I made answer: "It is because this sewer is unfit for human habitation. It is because you are all one gigantic mistake,—you and your monuments and your

merchants and everything about you. I rejoice to think
that scores of lakhs of rupees have been spent on public
offices at a place called Simla, that scores and scores will
be spent on the Delhi-Kalka line, in order that civilised
people may go there in comfort. When that line is
opened, your big city will be dead and buried and done
with, and I hope it will teach you a lesson. Your city
will rot, Sir." And he said: "When people are buried
here, they turn into adipocere in five days if the weather
is rainy. They saponify, you know." I said: "Go and
saponify, for I hate Calcutta." But he took me to the
Eden Gardens instead, and begged me for my own
sake not to go round the world in this prejudiced
spirit. I was unhappy and ill, but he vowed that my
spleen was due to my "Simla way of looking at things."

All this world of ours knows something about the
Eden Gardens, which are supposed by the uninitiated of
the mofussil to represent the gilded luxury of the me-
tropolis. As a matter of fact they are hideously dull.
The inhabitants appear in top-hats and frock-coats, and
walk dolorously to and fro under the glare of jerking
electric lamps, when they ought to be sitting in their
shirt-sleeves round little tables and treating their wives
to iced lager beer. My friend — it was a muggy
March night — wrapped himself in the prescribed
garments and said graciously: "You can wear a round
hat, but you mustn't wear deck-shoes; and for goodness'
sake, my dear fellow, don't smoke on the Red Road —
all the people one knows go there." Most of the
people who were people sat in their carriages, in an
atmosphere of hot horse, harness, and panel-lacquer,
outside the gardens, and the remnant tramped up and

down, by twos and threes, upon squashy green grass, until they were wearied, while a band played at them "And is this all you do?" I asked. "It is," said my friend. "Isn't it good enough? We meet every one we know here, and walk with him or her, unless he or she is among the carriages."

Overhead was a woolly warm sky; underfoot feverish soft grass; and from all quarters the languorous breeze bore faint reminiscences of stale sewage upon its wings. Round the horizon were stacked lines of carriages, and the electric flare bred aches in the strained eyebrow. It was a strange sight and fascinating. The doomed creatures walked up and down without cessation, for when one fled away into the lamp-spangled gloom twenty came to take his place. Slop-hatted members of the mercantile marine, Armenian merchants, Bengal civilians, shop-girls and shop-men, Jews, Parthians, and Mesopotamians, were all there in the tepid heat and the fetid smell.

"This," said my friend, "is how we enjoy ourselves. There are the Viceregal liveries. Lady Lansdowne comes here." He spoke as though reading to me the Government House list of Paradise. I reflected that these people would continue to walk up and down until they died, drinkless, dusty, sad, and blanched.

In saying this last thing I had made a mistake. Calcutta is no more Anglo-Indian than West Brompton. In common with Bombay, it has achieved a mental attitude several decades in advance of that of the raw and brutal India of fact. An intelligent and responsible financier, discussing the Empire, said: "But why do we want so large an army in India?   Look at the country all about."

I think he meant as far as the Circular Road or perhaps Raneegunge. Some of these days, when the voice of the two uncomprehending cities carries to London, and its advice is acted upon, there will be trouble. Till this second journey to Calcutta I was unable to account for the acid tone and limited range of the Presidency journals. I see now that they are ward papers and ought to be treated as such.

In the fulness of time — there was no hurry — imagine that, O you toilers of the land — I took ship and fled from Calcutta by that which they call the Mutton-Mail, because it takes sheep and correspondence to Rangoon. Half the Punjab was going with us to serve the Queen in the Burma Military Police, and it was grateful to catch once more the raw, rasping up-country speech amid the jabber of Burmese and Bengali.

To Rangoon, then, aboard the *Madura*, come with me down the Hughli, and try to understand what sort of life is led by the pilots, those strange men who only seem to know the land by watching it from the river.

"And I fetched up under the north ridge with six inches o' water under me, with a sou'west monsoon blowing, an' me not knowing any more than the dead where in — Paradise — I was taking her," says one deep voice.

"Well, what do you expect?" says another. "They ought not all to be occulting lights. Give me a red with two flashes for outlying danger anyhow. The Hughli's the worst river in the world. Why, off the Lower Gasper only last year . . . "

"And look at the way Government treats you!"

The Hughli pilot is human. He may talk Greek in

the exercise of his profession, but he can unite at swearing at the Government as thoroughly as though he were an uncovenanted civilian. His life is a hard one; but he is full of strange stories, and when treated with proper respect may condescend to tell some of them. If he has served on the river for six years as a "cub," and is neither dead nor decrepit, I believe he can earn as much as fifty rupees by sending two thousand tons of ship and a few hundred souls flying down the reaches at twelve miles an hour. Then he drops over the side with your last love-letters and wanders about the estuary in a tug until he finds another steamer and brings her up. It does not take much to comfort him.

*   *   *   *   *   *   *

Somewhere in the open sea some days later. I give it up. I *cannot* write, and to sleep I am not ashamed. A glorious idleness has taken entire possession of me; journalism is an imposture; so is Literature; so is Art. All India dropped out of sight yesterday, and the rocking pilot-brig at the Sandheads bore my last message to the prison that I quit. We have reached blue water — crushed sapphire — and a little breeze is bellying the awning. Three flying-fish were sighted this morning; the tea at *chota-hazri* is not nice, but the captain is excellent. Is this budget of news sufficiently exciting, or must I in strict confidence tell you the story of the Professor and the compass? You will hear more about the Professor later, if, indeed, I ever touch pen again. When he was in India he worked about nine hours a day. At noon to-day he conceived an interest in cyclones and things of that kind — would go to his cabin to get a compass and a meteorological book. He went, but stopped to reflect by the brink of a drink. "The compass is in a box," said he, drowsily, "but the nuisance of it is that to get it I shall have to pull the box out from under my berth. All things considered, I don't think it's worth while." He loafed on deck, and I think by this time is fast asleep. There was no trace of shame in his voice for his mighty sloth. I would have reproved him, but the words died on my tongue. I was guiltier than he.

"Professor," said I, "there is a foolish little paper in Allahabad called the *Pioneer*. I am supposed to be writing it a letter — a letter with my hands! Did you ever hear of anything so absurd?"

"I wonder if Angostura bitters really go with whisky," said the Professor, toying with the neck of the bottle.

There is no such place as India; there never was a daily paper called the *Pioneer*. It was all a weary dream. The only real things in the world are crystal seas, clean-swept decks, soft rugs, warm sunshine, the smell of salt in the air, and fathomless, futile indolence.

THE RIVER OF THE LOST FOOTSTEPS AND THE GOLDEN
MYSTERY UPON ITS BANKS. THE INIQUITY OF JORDAN·
SHOWS HOW A MAN MAY GO TO THE SHWAY DAGON
PAGODA AND SEE IT NOT AND TO THE PEGU CLUB AND
HEAR TOO MUCH. A DISSERTATION ON MIXED DRINKS.

> "I am a part of all that I have met,
>   Yet all experience is an arch where through
>   Gleams that untravelled world whose margin fades
>   For ever and for ever when I move."

THERE was a river and a bar, a pilot and a great deal
of nautical mystery, and the Captain said the journey
from Calcutta was ended and that we should be in Rangoon in a few hours. It is not an impressive stream,
being low-banked, scrubby, and muddy; but as we gave
the staggering rice-boats the go-by, I reflected that I was
looking upon the River of the Lost Footsteps — the road
that so many, many men of my acquaintance had trav·
elled, never to return, within the past three years. Such
a one had gone up to open out Upper Burma, and had
himself been opened out by a Burmese dah in the cruel
scrub beyond Minhla; such another had gone to rule the
land in the Queen's name, but could not rule a hill stream
and was carried down under his horse. One had been
shot by his servant; another by a dacoit while he sat at
dinner; and a pitifully long list had found in jungle

fever their sole reward for "the difficulties and privations inseparably connected with military service," as the Bengal Army Regulations put it. I ran over half a score of names — policemen, subalterns, young civilians, employés of big trading firms, and adventurers. They had gone up the river and they had died. At my elbow stood one of the workers in New Burma, going to report himself at Rangoon, and he told tales of interminable chases after evasive dacoits, of marchings and counter-marchings that came to nothing, and of deaths in the wilderness as noble as they were sad.

Then, a golden mystery upheaved itself on the horizon — a beautiful winking wonder that blazed in the sun, of a shape that was neither Muslim dome nor Hindu temple spire. It stood upon a green knoll, and below it were lines of warehouses, sheds, and mills. Under what new god, thought I, are we irrepressible English sitting now?

"There's the old Shway Dagon" (pronounced Dagone, *not* like the god in the Scriptures), said my companion. "Confound it!" But it was not a thing to be sworn at. It explained in the first place why we took Rangoon, and in the second why we pushed on to see what more of rich or rare the land held. Up till that sight my uninstructed eyes could not see that the land differed much in appearance from the Sunderbuns, but the golden dome said: "This is Burma, and it will be quite unlike any land you know about." "It's a famous old shrine o' sorts," said my companion, "and now the Tounghoo-Mandalay line is open, pilgrims are flocking down by the thousand to see it. It lost its big gold top — 'thing that they call a *'htee* — in an earthquake: that's why it's all hidden by bamboo

work for a third of its height.   You should see it when
it's all uncovered.   They're regilding it now."

Why is it that when one views for the first time any of
the wonders of the earth a bystander always strikes in
with, "You should see it, etc."?   Such men given twenty
minutes from the tomb at the Day of Judgment, would
patronize the naked souls as they hurried up with the
glare of Tophet on their faces, and say: "You should
have seen this when Gabriel first began to blow."
What the Shway Dagon really is and how many books
may have been written upon its history and archæology
is no part of my business.   As it stood overlooking everything it seemed to explain all about Burma—why the
boys had gone north and died, why the troopers bustled
to and fro, and why the steamers of the Irrawaddy Flotilla
lay like black-backed gulls upon the water.

Then we came to a new land, and the first thing that
one of the regular residents said was: "This place isn't
India at all.   They ought to have made it a Crown colony."   Judging the Empire as it ought to be judged, by
its most prominent points — *videlicet*, its smells — he was
right; for though there is one stink in Calcutta, another
in Bombay, and a third and most pungent one in the
Punjab, yet they have a kinship of stinks, whereas Burma
smells quite otherwise.   It is not exactly what China
ought to smell like, but it is not India.   "What is it?"
I asked; and the man said " *Napi*," which is fish pickled
when it ought to have been buried long ago.   This food,
in guide-book language, is inordinately consumed by . . .
but everybody who has been within downwind range of
Rangoon knows what *napi* means, and those who do not
will not understand.

Yes, it was a very new land — a land where the people understood colour — a delightfully lazy land full of pretty girls and very bad cheroots.

The worst of it was that the Anglo-Indian was a foreigner, a creature of no account. He did not know Burman, — which was no great loss, — and the Madrassi insisted upon addressing him in English. The Madrassi, by the way, is a great institution. He takes the place of the Burman, who will not work, and in a few years returns to his native coast with rings on his fingers and bells on his toes. The consequences are obvious. The Madrassi demands, and receives, enormous wages, and gets to know that he is indispensable. The Burman exists beautifully, while his women-folk marry the Madrassi and the Chinaman, because these support them in affluence. When the Burman wishes to work he gets a Madrassi to do it for him. How he finds the money to pay the Madrassi I was not informed, but all men were agreed in saying that under no circumstances will the Burman exert himself in the paths of honest industry. Now, if a bountiful Providence had clothed you in a purple, green, amber or puce petticoat, had thrown a rose-pink scarf-turban over your head, and had put you in a pleasant damp country where rice grew of itself and fish came up to be caught, putrified and pickled, would *you* work? Would you not rather take a cheroot and loaf about the streets seeing what was to be seen? If two-thirds of your girls were grinning, good-humoured little maidens and the remainder positively pretty, would you not spend your time in making love?

The Burman does both these things, and the Englishman, who after all worked himself to Burma, says hard

things about him.   Personally I love the Burman with
the blind favouritism born of first impression.   When I
die I will be a Burman, with twenty yards of real King's
silk, that has been made in Mandalay, about my body,
and a succession of cigarettes between my lips.   I will
wave the cigarette to emphasise my conversation, which
shall be full of jest and repartee, and I will always walk
about with a pretty almond-coloured girl who shall laugh
and jest too, as a young maiden ought.   She shall not
pull a sari over her head when a man looks at her and
glare suggestively from behind it, nor shall she tramp
behind me when I walk: for these are the customs of
India.   She shall look all the world between the eyes, in
honesty and good fellowship, and I will teach her not to
defile her pretty mouth with chopped tobacco in a cab-
bage leaf, but to inhale good cigarettes of Egypt's best
brand.

Seriously, the Burmese girls are very pretty, and
when I saw them I understood much that I had heard
about — about our army in Flanders let us say.

Providence really helps those who do not help themselves.   I went up a street, name unknown, attracted by
the colour that was so wantonly flashed down its length.
There is colour in Rajputana and in Southern India, and
you can find a whole paletteful of raw tints at any down-
country durbar; but the Burmese way of colouring is
different.   With the women the scarf, petticoat, and
jacket are of three lively hues, and with the men putso
and head-wrap are gorgeous.   Thus you get your colours
dashed down in dots against a background of dark timber houses set in green foliage.   There are no canons of
art anywhere, and every scheme of colouring depends on

the power of the sun above. That is why men in a Lon
don fog do still believe in pale greens and sad reds.
Give me lilac, pink, vermilion, lapis lazuli, and blistering
blood red under fierce sunlight that mellows and modi-
fies all. I had just made this discovery and was noting
that the people treated their cattle kindly, when the
driver of an absurd little hired carriage built to the scale
of a fat Burma pony, volunteered to take me for a drive,
and we drove in the direction of the English quarter of
the town where the sahibs live in dainty little houses
made out of the sides of cigar boxes. They looked as if
they could be kicked in at a blow and (trust a Globe-
trotter for evolving a theory at a minute's notice) it is
to avoid this fate that they are built for the most
part on legs. The houses are not cantonment bred in
any way — nor did the uneven ground and dusty reddish roads fit in with any part of the Indian Empire
except it may be Ootacamund.

The pony wandered into a garden studded with
lovely little lakes which, again, were studded with
islands, and there were sahibs in flannels in the boats.
Outside the park were pleasant little monasteries full of
clean-shaved gentlemen in gold amber robes learning to
renounce the world, the flesh, and the devil by chatting
furiously amongst themselves, and at every corner stood
the three little maids from school, almost exactly as they
had been dismissed from the side scenes of the Savoy after
the *Mikado* was over: and the strange part of it all was
that every one laughed — laughed, so it seemed, at the sky
above them because it was blue, at the sun because it was
sinking, and at each other because they had nothing better
to do. A small fat child laughed loudest of all, in spite

of the fact that it was smoking a cheroot that ought to
have made it deathly sick.   The pagoda was always close
at hand — as brilliant a mystery as when first sighted far
down the river; but it changed its shape as we came
nearer, and showed in the middle of a nest of hundreds of
smaller pagodas.   There appeared suddenly two colossal
tigers (after the Burmese canons) in plaster on a hillside,
and they were the guardians of Burma's greatest pagoda.
Round them rustled a great crowd of happy people in
pretty dresses, and the feet of all were turned towards a
great stoneway that ran from between the tigers even to
the brow of the mound.   But the nature of the stairs was
peculiar.   They were covered in for the most part by a
tunnel, or it may have been a walled-in colonnade, for
there were heavily gilt wooden pillars visible in the
gloom.   The afternoon was drawing on as I came to this
strange place and saw that I should have to climb up a
long, low hill of stairs to get to the pagoda.

Once or twice in my life I have seen a Globe-trotter
literally gasping with jealous emotion because India was
so much larger and more lovely than he had ever
dreamed, and because he had only set aside three
months to explore it in.   My own sojourn in Rangoon
was countable by hours, so I may be forgiven when I
pranced with impatience at the bottom of the staircase
because I could not at once secure a full, complete, and
accurate idea of everything that was to be seen.   The
meaning of the guardian tigers, the inwardness of the
main pagoda, and the countless little ones, was hidden
from me.   I could not understand why the pretty girls
with cheroots sold little sticks and coloured candles to
be used before the image of Buddha.   Everything was

incomprehensible to me, and there was none to explain.
All that I could gather was that in a few days the
great golden 'htee that has been defaced by the earthquake would be hoisted into position with feasting
and song, and that half Upper Burma was coming
down to see the show.

I went forward between the two great beasts, across
a whitewashed court, till I came to a flat-headed arch
guarded by the lame, the blind, the leper, and the de-
formed. These plucked at my clothes as I passed, and
moaned and whined: but the stream that disappeared
up the gentle slope of the stairway took no notice of
them. And I stepped into the semi-darkness of a long,
long corridor flanked by booths, and floored with stones
worn very smooth by human feet.

At the far end of the roofed corridor there was a
breadth of evening sky, and at this point rose a second
and much steeper flight of stairs, leading directly to the
Shwedagon (this, by the way, is its real spelling). Down
this staircase fell, from gloom to deeper gloom, a cas-
cade of colour. At this point I stayed, because there
was a beautiful archway of Burmese build, and adorned
with a Chinese inscription, directly in front of me, and
I conceived foolishly that I should find nothing more
pleasant to look at if I went farther. Also, I wished
to understand how such a people could produce the dacoit of the newspaper, and I knew that a great deal of
promiscuous knowledge comes to him who sits down by
the wayside. Then I saw a Face—which explained a
good deal. The chin, jowl, lips, and neck were modelled
faithfully on the lines of the worst of the Roman Em-
presses—the lolloping, walloping women that Swin-

burne sings about, and that we sometimes see pictures of. Above this gross perfection of form came the Mongoloid nose, narrow forehead, and flaring pig's eyes. I stared intently, and the man stared back again, with admirable insolence, that puckered one corner of his mouth Then he swaggered forward, and I was richer by a new face and a little knowledge. "I must make further inquiries at the Club," said I, "but that man seems to be of the proper dacoit type. He could crucify on occasion."

Then a brown baby came by in its mother's arms and laughed, wherefore I much desired to shake hands with it, and grinned to that effect. The mother held out the tiny soft pud and laughed, and the baby laughed, and we all laughed together, because that seemed to be the custom of the country, and returned down the now dark corridor where the lamps of the stall-keepers were twinkling and scores of people were helping us to laugh. They must be a mild-mannered nation, the Burmese, for they leave little three-year-olds in charge of a whole wilderness of clay dolls or a menagerie of jointed tigers.

I had not actually entered the Shwedagon, but I felt just as happy as though I had.

In the Pegu Club I found a friend — a Punjabi — upon whose broad bosom I threw myself and demanded food and entertainment. He had not long since received a visit from the Commissioner of Peshawar, of all places in the world, and was not to be upset by sudden arrivals. But he had come down in the world hideously. Years ago in the Black North he used to speak the vernacular as it should be spoken, and was one of us.

"*Daniel, how many socks master got?*"

The unfinished peg fell from my fist. "Good Heavens!" said I, "is it possible that you — you — speak that disgusting pidgin-talk to your *nauker* ? It's enough to make one cry. You're no better than a Bombaywallah."

"I'm a Madrassi," said he, calmly. "We all talk English to our boys here. Isn't it beautiful? Now come along to the Gymkhana and then we'll dine here. Daniel, master's hat and stick get."

There must be a few hundred men who are fairly behind the scenes of the Burma War — one of the least known and appreciated of any of our little affairs. The Pegu Club seemed to be full of men on their way up or down, and the conversation was but an echo of the murmur of conquest far away to the north.

"See that man over there. He was cut over the head the other day at Zoungloung-goo. Awfully tough man. That chap next him has been on the dacoit-hunt for about a year. He broke up Boh Mango's gang : caught the Boh in a paddy field, y'know. The other man's going home on sick leave — got a lump of iron somewhere in his system. Try our mutton : I assure you the Club is the only place in Rangoon where you get mutton. Look here, you must *not* speak vernacular to our boys. Hi, boy ! get master some more ice. They're all Bombay men or Madrassis. Up at the front there are some Burman servants : but a real Burman will never work. He prefers being a simple little *daku*."

"How much ? "

"Dear little dacoit. We call 'em *dakus* for short — sort o' pet name. That's the butter-fish. I forgot you didn't get much fish up-country. Yes, I s'pose Rangoon has its advantages. You pay like a Prince. Take an

ordinary married establishment. Little furnished house
— one hundred and fifty rupees. Servants' wages two
twenty or two fifty. That's four hundred at once. My
dear fellow, a sweeper won't take less than twelve or sixteen rupees a month here, and even then he'll work for
other houses. It's worse than Quetta. Any man who
comes to Lower Burma in the hope of living on his pay
is a fool."

Voice from lower end of table. "Dee fool. It's different in Upper Burma, where you get command and travelling allowances."

Another voice in the middle of a conversation. "They
never got that story into the papers, but I can tell you
we weren't quite as quick in rushing the fort as they
made believe. You see Boh Gwee had us in a regular
trap, and by the time we had closed the line our men
were being peppered front and rear: that jungle-fighting
is the deuce and all. More ice please."

Then they told me of the death of an old school-fellow
under the ramp of the Minhla redoubt — does any one
remember the affair at Minhla that opened the third
Burmese ball?

"I was close to him," said a voice. "He died in A.'s
arms, I fancy, but I'm not quite sure. Anyhow, I know
he died easily. He was a good fellow."

"Thank you," said I, "and now I think I'll go; " and
I went out into the steamy night, my head ringing with
stories of battle, murder, and sudden death. I had
reached the fringe of the veil that hides Upper Burma,
and I would have given much to have gone up the river
and seen a score of old friends, now jungle-worn men of
war. All that night I dreamed of interminable staircases

down which swept thousands of pretty girls, so brill-
iantly robed that my eyes ached at the sight. There was
a great golden bell at the top of the stairs, and at the
bottom, his face turned to the sky, lay poor old D——
dead at Minhla, and a host of unshaven ragamuffins in
khaki were keeping guard over him.

THE CITY OF ELEPHANTS WHICH IS GOVERNED BY THE
GREAT GOD OF IDLENESS, WHO LIVES ON THE TOP OF
A HILL.   THE HISTORY OF THREE GREAT DISCOVERIES
AND THE NAUGHTY CHILDREN OF IQUIQUE.

> "I built my soul a lordly pleasure-house
> Wherein at ease for aye to dwell,
> I said: Oh, soul, make merry and carouse,
> Dear soul, for all is well."

So much for making definite programmes of travel
beforehand.   In my first letter I told you that I would
go from Rangoon to Penang direct.   Now we are lying
off Moulmein in a new steamer which does not seem
to run anywhere in particular.   Why she should go to
Moulmein is a mystery; but as every soul on the ship
is a loafer like myself, no one is discontented.   Imagine
a shipload of people to whom time is no object, who
have no desires beyond three meals a day and no
emotions save those caused by a casual cockroach.

Moulmein is situated up the mouth of a river which
ought to flow through South America, and all manner
of dissolute native craft appear to make the place
their home.   Ugly cargo-steamers that the initiated
call "Geordie tramps" grunt and bellow at the beautiful hills all round, and the pot-bellied British India
liners wallow down the reaches.   Visitors are rare in

Moulmein — so rare that few but cargo-boats think it
worth their while to come off from the shore.

Strictly in confidence I will tell you that Moulmein
is not a city of this earth at all. Sindbad the Sailor
visited it, if you recollect, on that memorable voyage
when he discovered the burial-ground of the elephants.

As the steamer came up the river we were aware of
first one elephant and then another hard at work in
timber-yards that faced the shore. A few narrow-
minded folk with binoculars said that there were
mahouts upon their backs, but this was never clearly
proven. I prefer to believe in what I saw — a sleepy
town, just one house thick, scattered along a lovely
stream and inhabited by slow, solemn elephants, building stockades for their own diversion. There was a
strong scent of freshly sawn teak in the air — we could
not see any elephants sawing — and occasionally the
warm stillness was broken by the crash of the log.
When the elephants had got an appetite for luncheon
they loafed off in couples to their club, and did not
take the trouble to give us greeting and the latest mail
papers ; at which we were much disappointed, but took
heart when we saw upon a hill a large white pagoda
surrounded by scores of little pagodas. "This," we
said with one voice, "is the place to make an excur-
sion to," and then shuddered at our own profanity,
for above all things we did not wish to behave like
mere vulgar tourists.

The *ticca-gharies* at Moulmein are three sizes smaller
than those of Rangoon, as the ponies are no bigger than
decent sheep. Their drivers trot them uphill and down,
and as the *ghari* is extremely narrow and the roads are

anything but good, the exercise is refreshing. Here again all the drivers are Madrassis.

I should better remember what that pagoda was like had I not fallen deeply and irrevocably in love with a Burmese girl at the foot of the first flight of steps. Only the fact of the steamer starting next noon prevented me from staying at Moulmein forever and owning a pair of elephants. These are so common that they wander about the streets, and, I make no doubt, could be obtained for a piece of sugar-cane.

Leaving this far too lovely maiden, I went up the steps only a few yards, and, turning me round, looked upon a view of water, island, broad river, fair grazing ground, and belted wood that made me rejoice that I was alive. The hillside below me and above me was ablaze with pagodas — from a gorgeous golden and vermilion beauty to a delicate grey stone one just completed in honour of an eminent priest lately deceased at Mandalay. Far above my head there was a faint tinkle, as of golden bells, and a talking of the breezes in the tops of the toddy-palms. Wherefore I climbed higher and higher up the steps till I reached a place of great peace, dotted with Burmese images, spotlessly clean. Here women now and again paid reverence. They bowed their heads and their lips moved, because they were praying. I had an umbrella — a black one — in my hand, deck-shoes upon my feet, and a helmet upon my head. I did not pray — I swore at myself for being a Globe-trotter, and wished that I had enough Burmese to explain to these ladies that I was sorry and would have taken off my hat but for the sun. A Globe-trotter is a brute. I had the grace to blush as I tramped round the pagoda. That will be remembered to me for righteousness. But I stared horribly — at a gold and red side-temple with a beautifully gilt image of Buddha in it — at the grim figures in the niches at the base of the main pagoda — at the little palms that grew out of the cracks in the tiled paving of the court — at the big palms above, and at the low hung bronze bells that stood at each corner for the women to smite with stag-horns. Upon one bell rang this amazing triplet in English, evidently the composition of the caster, who completed his work — and now, let us hope, has reached Nibban — thirty-five years ago: —

> " He who destroyed this Bell
> They must be in the great Hel
> And unable to coming out."

I respect a man who is not able to spell Hell properly. It shows that he has been brought up in an amiable creed. You who come to Moulmein treat this bell with respect, and refrain from playing with it, for that hurts the feelings of the worshippers.

In the base of the pagoda were four rooms, lined as to three sides with colossal plaster figures, before each of whom burned one solitary dip whose rays fought with the flood of evening sunshine that came through the windows, and the room was filled with a pale yellow light — unearthly to stand in. Occasionally a woman crept in to one of these rooms to pray, but nearly all the company stayed in the courtyard; but those that faced the figures prayed more zealously than the others, so I judged that their troubles were the greater. Of the actual cult I knew less than nothing; for the neatly

bound English books that we read make no mention
of pointing red-tipped straws at a golden image, or of
the banging of bells after the custom of worshippers in
a Hindu temple. It must be a genial one, however. To
begin with, it is quiet and carried on among the fairest
possible surroundings that ever landscape offered.

In this particular case, the massive white pagoda shot
into the blue from the west of a walled hill that commanded
four separate and desirable views as you looked either
at the steamer in the river below, the polished silver
reaches to the left, the woods to the right, or the roofs
of Moulmein to the landward. Between each pause of
the rustling of dresses and the low-toned talk of the
women fell, from far above, the tinkle of innumerable
metal leaves which were stirred by the breeze as they
hung from the '*htee* of the pagoda. A golden image
winked in the sun; the painted ones stared straight in
front of them over the heads of the worshippers, and
somewhere below a mallet and a plane were lazily helping to build yet another pagoda in honour of the Lord
of the Earth.

Sitting in meditation while the Professor went round
with a sacrilegious camera, to the vast terror of the Burmese youth, I made two notable discoveries and nearly
went to sleep over them. The first was that the Lord
of the Earth is Idleness — thick slab idleness with a
little religion stirred in to keep it sweet, and the second
was that the shape of the pagoda came originally from a
bulging toddy-palm trunk. There was one between me
and the far-off sky line, and it exactly duplicated the
outlines of a small grey stone building.

Yet a third discovery, and a much more important one,

came to me later on. A dirty little imp of a boy ran by clothed more or less in a beautifully worked silk putso, the like of which I had in vain attempted to secure at Rangoon. A bystander told me that such an article would cost one hundred and ten rupees — exactly ten rupees in excess of the price demanded at Rangoon, when I had been discourteous to a pretty Burmese girl with diamonds in her ears, and had treated her as though she were a Delhi boxwallah.

"Professor," said I, when the camera spidered round the corner, "there is something wrong with this people. They won't work, they aren't all dacoits, and their babies run about with hundred-rupees putsoes on them, while their parents speak the truth. How in the world do they get a living?"

"They exist beautifully," said the Professor; "and I only brought half a dozen plates with me. I shall come again in the morning with some more. Did I ever dream of a place like this?"

"No," said I. "It's perfect, and for the life of me I can't quite see where the precise charm lies."

"In its Beastly Laziness," said the Professor, as he packed the camera, and we went away, regretfully, haunted by the voices of many wind-blown bells.

Not ten minutes from the pagoda we saw a real British bandstand, a shanty labelled "Municipal Office," a collection of P. W. D. bungalows that in vain strove to blast the landscape, and a Madras band. I had never seen Madrassi troops before. They seem to dress just like Tommies, and have an air of much culture and refinement. It is said that they read English books and know all about their rights and privileges. For further details apply to the Pegu Club, second table from the top on the right hand side as you enter.

In an evil hour I attempted to revive the drooping trade of Moulmein, and to this end bound a native of the place to come on board the steamer next morn with a collection of Burmese silks. It was only a five minutes' pull, and he could have sat in the stern all the while. Morning came, but not the man. Not a boat of watermelons, pink fleshy watermelons, neared the ship. We might have been in quarantine. As we slipped down the river on our way to Penang, I saw the elephants playing with the teak logs as solemnly and as mysteriously as ever. They were the chief inhabitants, and, for aught I know, the rulers of the place. Their lethargy had corrupted the town, and when the Professor wished to photograph them, I believe they went away in scorn.

We are now running down to Penang with the thermometer 87° in the cabins, and anything you please on deck. We have exhausted all our literature, drunk two hundred lemon squashes, played forty different games of cards (Patience mostly), organised a lottery on the run (had it been a thousand rupees instead of ten I should not have won it), and slept seventeen hours out of the twenty-four. It is perfectly impossible to write, but you may be morally the better for the story of the Bad People of Iquique which, "as you have not before heard, I will now proceed to relate." It has just been told me by a German orchid-hunter, fresh from nearly losing his head in the Lushai hills, who has been over most of the world.

Iquique is somewhere in South America — at the back

of or beyond Brazil — and once upon a time there came to it a tribe of Aborigines from out of the woods, so innocent that they wore nothing at all — absolutely nothing at all. They had a grievance, but no garments, and the former they came to lay before His Excellency, the Governor of Iquique. But the news of their coming and their exceeding nakedness had gone before them, and good Spanish ladies of the town agreed that the heathen should first of all be clothed. So they organised a sewing-bee, and the result, which was mainly aprons, was served out to the Bad People with hints as to its use. Nothing could have been better. They appeared in their aprons before the Governor and all the ladies of Iquique, ranged on the steps of the cathedral, only to find that the Governor could not grant their demands. And do you know what these children of nature did? In the twinkling of an eye they had off those aprons, slung them round their necks, and were dancing naked as the dawn before the scandalised ladies of Iquique, who fled with their fans before their eyes into the sanctuary of the cathedral. And when the steps were deserted the Bad People withdrew, shouting and leaping, their aprons still round their necks, for good cloth is valuable property. They encamped near the town, knowing their own power. 'Twas impossible to send the military against them, and equally impossible that Donnas and Señoritas should be exposed to the chance of being shocked whenever they went abroad. No one knew at what hour the Bad People would sweep through the streets. Their demands were therefore granted and Iquique had rest. Nuda est veritas et prevalebit.

"But," said I, "what is there so awful in a naked

Indian — or two hundred naked Indians for that matter?"

"My friend," said the German, "dey vas Indians of
Sout' America. I dell you dey do not demselves shtrip
vell."

I put my hand on my mouth and went away.

SHOWING HOW I CAME TO PALMISTE ISLAND AND THE PLACE OF PAUL AND VIRGINIA, AND FELL ASLEEP IN A GARDEN. A DISQUISITION ON THE FOLLY OF SIGHT-SEEING.

> " Some for the glories of this world and some
> Sigh for the Prophet's paradise to come.
> Ah, take the cash and let the credit go,
> Nor heed the rumble of a distant drum."

THERE is something very wrong in the Anglo-Saxon character. Hardly had the *Africa* dropped anchor in Penang Straits when two of our fellow-passengers were smitten with madness because they heard that another steamer was even then starting for Singapur. If they went by it they would gain several days. Heaven knows why time should have been so precious to them. The news sent them flying into their cabins, and packing their trunks as though their salvation depended upon it. Then they tumbled over the side and vere rowed away in a sampan, hot, but happy. They were on a pleasure-trip, and they had gained perhaps three days. That was their pleasure.

Do you recollect Besant's description of Palmiste Island in *My Little Girl* and *So They Were Married?* Penang is Palmiste Island. I found this out from

the ship, looking at the wooded hills that dominate
the town, and at the regiments of palm trees three
miles away that marked the coast of Wellesley Prov-
ince. The air was soft and heavy with laziness, and
at the ship's side were boat-loads of much jewelled
Madrassis — even those to whom Besant has alluded.
A squall swept across the water and blotted out the
rows of low, red-tiled houses that made up Penang, and
the shadows of night followed the storm.

I put my twelve-inch rule in my pocket to measure all
the world by, and nearly wept with emotion when on
landing at the jetty I fell against a Sikh — a beautiful
bearded Sikh, with white leggings and a rifle. As is
cold water in a thirsty land so is a face from the old
country. My friend had come from Jandiala in the
Umritsar district. Did I know Jandiala? Did I
not? I began to tell all the news I could recollect about crops and armies and the movements of
big men in the far, far north while the Sikh beamed.
He belonged to the military police, and it was a good
service, but of course it was far from the old country.
There was no hard work, and the Chinamen gave but
little trouble. They had fights among themselves, but
"they do not care to give us any impudence;" and the
big man swaggered off with the long roll and swing of
a whole Pioneer regiment, while I cheered myself with
the thought that India — the India I pretend to hold in
hatred — was not so far off, after all.

You know our ineradicable tendency to damn everything in the mofussil. Calcutta professes astonishment
that Allahabad has a good dancing floor; Allahabad
wonders if it is true that Lahore really has an ice-fac-

tory; and Lahore pretends to believe that everybody in Peshawar sleeps armed. Very much in the same way I was amused at seeing a steam tramway in Rangoon, and after we had quitted Moulmein fully expected to find the outskirts of civilisation. Vanity and ignorance were severely shocked when they confronted a long street of business — a street of two-storied houses, full of *ticca-gharies*, shop signs, and above all *jinrickshaws*.

You in India have never seen a proper *'rickshaw*. There are about two thousand of them in Penang, and no two seem alike. They are lacquered with bold figures of dragons and horses and birds and butterflies: their shafts are of black wood bound with white metal, and so strong that the coolie sits upon them when he waits for his fare. There is only one coolie, but he is strong, and he runs just as well as six bell-men. He ties up his pigtail, — being a Cantonese, — and this is a disadvantage to sahibs who cannot speak Tamil, Malay, or Cantonese. Otherwise he might be steered like a camel.

The *'rickshaw* men are patient and long-suffering. The evil-visaged person who drove my carriage lashed at them when they came within whip range, and did his best to drive over them as he headed for the Waterfalls, which are five miles away from Penang Town. I expected that the buildings should stop, choked out among the dense growth of cocoanut. But they continued for many streets, very like Park and Middleton streets in Calcutta, where shuttered houses, which were half-bred between an Indian bungalow and a Rangoon rabbit-hutch, fought with the greenery and crotons as big as small trees. Now and again there blazed the front of a Chinese house, all open-work vermilion, lamp-black, and gold, with six-foot

Chinese lanterns over the doorways and glimpses of
quaintly cut shrubs in the well-kept gardens beyond.

We struck into roads fringed with native houses
on piles, shadowed by the everlasting cocoanut palms
heavy with young nuts. The heat was heavy with
the smell of vegetation, and it was not the smell of
the earth after the rains. Some bird-thing called
out from the deeps of the foliage, and there was a
mutter of thunder in the hills which we were approach-
ing: but all the rest was very still — and the sweat ran
down our faces in drops.

"Now you've got to walk up that hill," said the driver.
pointing to a small barrier outside a well-kept botanical
garden; "all the carriages stop here." One's limbs moved
as though leaden, and the breath came heavily, drawing
in each time the vapour of a Turkish bath. The soil
was alive with wet and warmth, and the unknown trees
— I was too sleepy to read the labels that some offen-
sively energetic man has written — were wet and warm
too. Up on the hillside the voice of the water was saying something, but I was too sleepy to listen; and on the
top of the hill lay a fat cloud just like an eider-down
quilt tucking everything in safely.

> "And in the afternoon they came unto a land
> In which it seemed always afternoon."

I sat down where I was, for I saw that the upward path
was very steep and was cut into rude steps, and an exposition of sleep had come upon me. I was at the mouth
of a tiny gorge, exactly where the lotus-eaters had sat
down when they began their song, for I recognised the
Waterfall and the air round my ears "breathing as one
that has a weary dream."

I looked and beheld that I could not give in words the genius of the place. "I can't play the flute, but I have a cousin who plays the violin." I knew a man who could. Some people said he was not a nice man, and I might run the risk of contaminating morals, but nothing mattered in such a climate. See now, go to the very worst of Zola's novels and read there his description of a conservatory. That was it. Several months passed away, but there was neither chill nor burning heat to mark the passage of time. Only, with a sense of acute pain I felt that I must "do" the Waterfall, and I climbed up the steps in the hillside, though every boulder cried "sit down," until I found a small stream of water coursing down the face of a rock, and a much bigger one down my own.

Then we went away to breakfast, the stomach being always more worthy than any amount of sentiment. A turn in the road hid the gardens and stopped the noise of the waters, and that experience was over for all time. Experiences are very like cheroots. They generally begin badly, taste perfect half way through, and at the butt-end are things to be thrown away and never picked up again. . . .

His name was John, and he had a pigtail five feet long — all real hair and no silk braided, and he kept an hotel by the way and fed us with a chicken, into whose innocent flesh onions and strange vegetables had been forced. Till then we had feared Chinamen, especially when they brought food, but now we will eat anything at their hands. The conclusion of the meal was a half-guinea pineapple and a siesta. This is a beautiful thing which we of India — but I am of India no more — do not understand. You lie down and wait for time to pass. You

are not in the least wearied — and you would not go to
sleep. You are filled with a divine drowsiness — quite
different from the heavy sodden slumber of a hot-
weather Sunday, or the businesslike repose of a Europe
morning. Now I begin to despise novelists who write
about *siestas* in cold climates. I know what the real
thing means.

*   *   *   *   *   *   *

I have been trying to buy a few things — a *sarong*, which
is a *putso* which is a *dhoti;* a pipe; and a "damned Malay-
an kris." The *sarongs* come chiefly from Germany, the
pipes from the pawn-shops, and there are no krises except
little toothpick things that could not penetrate the hide
of a Malay. In the native town, I found a large army
of Chinese — more than I imagined existed in China itself
— encamped in spacious streets and houses, some of them
sending block-tin to Singapur, some driving fine carriages,
others making shoes, chairs, clothes, and every other thing
that a large town desires. They were the first army corps
on the march of the Mongol. The scouts are at Calcutta,
and a flying column at Rangoon. Here begins the main
body, some hundred thousand strong, so they say. Was
it not De Quincey that had a horror of the Chinese — of
their inhumaneness and their inscrutability? Certainly
the people in Penang are not nice; they are even terrible
to behold. They work hard, which in this climate is
manifestly wicked, and their eyes are just like the eyes
of their own pet dragons. Our Hindu gods are passable, some of them even jolly — witness our pot-bellied
Ganesh; but what can you do with a people who revel in
D T. monsters and crown their roof-ridges with flames of

fire, or the waves of the sea? They swarmed everywhere, and wherever three or four met, there they eat
things without name — the insides of ducks for choice.
Our deck passengers, I know, fared sumptuously on offal
begged from the steward and flavoured with insect-
powder to keep the ants off. This, again, is not natural,
for a man should eat like a man if he works like one. I
could quite understand after a couple of hours (this has
the true Globe-trotter twang to it) spent in Chinatown
why the lower-caste Anglo-Saxon hates the Celestial.
He frightened me, and so I could take no pleasure in
looking at his houses, at his wares, or at himself. . . .

The smell of printer's ink is marvellously penetrating.
It drew me up two pair of stairs into an office where the
exchanges lay about in delightful disorder, and a little
hand-press was clacking out proofs just in the old
sweet way. Something like the *Gazette of India* showed
that the Straits Settlements — even they — had a Government of their own, and I sighed for a dead past as my
eye caught the beautiful official phraseology that never
varies. How alike we English are! Here is an extract
from a report: "And the Chinese form of decoration
which formerly covered the office has been wisely oblit-
erated with whitewash."

That was just what I came to inquire about. What
were they going to do with the Chinese decoration all
over Penang? Would they try to wisely obliterate that?

The Straits Settlement Council which lives at Singapur
had just passed a Bill (Ordinance they call it) putting
down all Chinese secret societies in the colony, which
measure only awaited the Imperial assent. A little business in Singapur connected with some municipal meas

ure for clearing away overhanging verandahs created a
storm, and for three days those who were in the place
say the town was entirely at the mercy of the Chinese,
who rose all together and made life unpleasant for the
authorities. This incident forced the Government to take
serious notice of the secret societies who could so control
the actions of men, and the result has been a measure
which it will not be easy to enforce. A Chinaman *must*
have a secret society of some kind. He has been bred
up in a country where they were necessary to his comfort, his protection, and the maintenance of his scale of
wages from time immemorial, and he will carry them
with him as he will carry his opium and his coffin.

"Do you expect then that the societies will collapse
by proclamation?" I asked the editor.

"No. There will be a row."

"What row? what sort of a row?"

"More troops, perhaps, and perhaps some gunboats.
You see, we shall have Sir Charles Warren then as our
Commander-in-Chief at Singapur. Up till the present
our military administration has been subordinate to that
of Hong-Kong; when that is done away with and we
have Sir Charles Warren, things will be different. But
there will be a row. Neither you nor I nor any one else
will be able to put these things down. Every joss house
will be the head of a secret society. What can one do?
In the past the Government made some use of them for
the detection of crime. Now they are too big and too
important to be treated in that way. You will know
before long whether we have been able to suppress them.
There will be a row."

Certainly the great grievance of Penang is the Chinese

question. She would not be human did she not revile her Municipal Commissioners and talk about the unsanitary condition of the island. If nose and eyes and ears be any guide, she is far cleaner even in her streets than many an Indian cantonment, and her water-supply seems perfection. But I sat in that little newspaper office and listened to stories of municipal intrigue that might have suited Serampore or Calcutta, only the names were a little different, and in place of Ghose and Chuckerbutty one heard titles such as Yih Tat, Lo Eng, and the like. The Englishman's aggressive altruism always leads him to build towns for others, and incite aliens to serve on municipal boards. Then he gets tired of his weakness and starts papers to condemn himself. They had a Chinaman on the Municipality last year. They have now got rid of him, and the present body is constituted of two officials and four non-officials. *Therefore* they complain of the influence of officialdom.

Having thoroughly settled all the differences of Penang to my own great satisfaction, I removed myself to a Chinese theatre set in the open road, and made of sticks and old gunny-bags. The orchestra alone convinced me that there was something radically wrong with the Chinese mind. Once, long ago in Jummu, I heard the infernal clang of the horns used by the Devil-dancers who had come from far beyond Ladakh to do honour to the Prince that day set upon his throne. That was about three thousand miles to the north, but the character of the music was unchanged. A thousand Chinamen stood as close as possible to the horrid din and enjoyed it. Once more, can anything be done to a people without nerves as without digestion, and, if reports speak truly, without

morals? But it is not true that they are born with full-
sized pigtails. The thing grows, and in its very earliest
stages is the prettiest head-dressing imaginable, being
soft brown, very fluffy, about three inches long, and
dressed as to the end with red silk. An infant pigtail
is just like the first tender sprout of a tulip bulb, and
would be lovable were not the Chinese baby so very horrible of hue and shape. He isn't as pretty as the pig
that Alice nursed in Wonderland, and he lies quite still
and never cries. This is because he is afraid of being
boiled and eaten. I saw cold boiled babies on a plate
being carried through the heart of the town. They said
it was only sucking-pig, but I knew better. Dead sucking-
pigs don't grin with their eyes open.

About this time the faces of the Chinese frightened
me more than ever, so I ran away to the outskirts
of the town and saw a windowless house that carried
the Square and Compass in gold and teakwood above
the door. I took heart at meeting these familiar things
again, and knowing that where they were was good
fellowship and much charity, in spite of all the secret
societies in the world. Penang is to be congratulated
on one of the prettiest little lodges in the East.

No. V

OF THE THRESHOLD OF THE FAR EAST AND THE DWELLERS
THEREON.   A DISSERTATION UPON THE USE OF THE
BRITISH LION.

> " How the world is made for each of us,
> How all we perceive and know in it
> Tends to some moment's product — thus
> When a soul declares itself — to wit
> By its fruit, the thing it does."

"I ASSURE you, Sir, weather as hot as this has not
been felt in Singapur for years and years.   March is
always reckoned our hottest month, but this is quite
abnormal."

And I made answer to the stranger wearily: —

"Yes, of course.   They always told that lie in the
other places.   Leave me alone and let me drip."

This is the heat of an orchid-house, — a clinging, re-
morseless, steam-sweat that knows no variation between
night and day.   Singapur is another Calcutta, but much
more so.   In the suburbs they are building rows of cheap
houses; in the city they run over you and jostle you into
the kennel.   These are unfailing signs of commercial
prosperity.   India ended so long ago that I cannot even
talk about the natives of the place.   They are all Chinese,
except where they are French or Dutch or German.
England is by the uninformed supposed to own the

283

island. The rest belongs to China and the Continent, but chiefly China. I knew I had touched the borders of the Celestial Empire when I was thoroughly impregnated with the reek of Chinese tobacco, a fine-cut, greasy, glossy weed, to whose smoke the aroma of a huqa in the cookhouse is all Rimmell's shop.

Providence conducted me along a beach, in full view of five miles of shipping,—five solid miles of masts and funnels,—to a place called Raffles Hotel, where the food is as excellent as the rooms are bad. Let the traveller take note. Feed at Raffles and sleep at the Hotel de l'Europe. I would have done this but for the apparition of two large ladies tastefully attired in bed-gowns, who sat with their feet propped on a chair. This Joseph ran; but it turned out that they were Dutch ladies from Batavia, and that that was their national costume till dinner time.

"If, as you say, they had on stockings and dressing-gowns, you have nothing to complain of. They generally wear nothing but a night-gown till five o'clock," quoth a man versed in the habits of the land.

I do not know whether he spoke the truth; I am inclined to think that he did; but now I know what "Batavian grace" really means, I don't approve of it. A lady in a dressing-gown disturbs the mind and prevents careful consideration of the political outlook in Singapur, which is now supplied with a set of very complete forts, and is hopefully awaiting some nine-inch breach-loaders that are to adorn them. There is something very pathetic in the trustful, clinging attitude of the Colonies, who ought to have been soured and mistrustful long ago. "We hope the Home Government may do this. It is possible that the Home Government may do that," is the burden of the song, and in every place where the Englishman cannot breed successfully must continue to be. Imagine an India fit for permanent habitation by our kin, and consider what a place it would be this day, with the painter cut fifty years ago, fifty thousand miles of railways laid down and ten thousand under survey, and possibly an annual surplus. Is this sedition? Forgive me, but I am looking at the shipping outside the verandah, at the Chinamen in the streets, and at the lazy, languid Englishmen in banians and white jackets stretched on the cane chairs, and these things are not nice. The men are not really lazy, as I will try to show later on, but they lounge and loaf and seem to go to office at eleven, which must be bad for work. And they all talk about going home at indecently short intervals, as though that were their right. Once more, if we could only rear children that did not run to leg and nose in the second generation in this part of the world and one or two others, what an amazing disruption of the Empire there would be before half of a Parnell Commission sitting was accomplished ! And then, later, when the freed States had plunged into hot water, fought their fights, overborrowed, overspeculated, and otherwise conducted themselves like younger sons, what a coming together and revision of tariffs, ending in one great iron band girdling the earth. Within that limit free trade. Without, rancorous Protection. It would be too vast a hornet's nest for any combination of Powers to disturb. The dream will not come about for a long time, but we shall accomplish something like it one of these days. The birds of passage from Canada,

from Borneo,—Borneo that will have to go through a
general rough-and-tumble before she grips her possibilities,—from Australia, from a hundred scattered islands,
are saying the same thing: "We are not strong enough
yet, but some day We shall be."

Oh! dear people, stewing in India and swearing at all
the Governments, it is a glorious thing to be an Englishman. "Our lot has fallen unto us in a fair ground.
Yea, we have a goodly heritage." Take a map and
look at the long stretch of the Malay Peninsula,—a
thousand miles southerly it runs, does it not?—whereon
Penang, Malacca, and Singapur are so modestly under-
lined in red ink. See, now. We have our Residents at
every one of the Malay native States of any importance,
and right up the line to Kedah and Siam our influence
regulates and controls all. Into this land God put
first gold and tin, and after these the Englishman, who
floats companies, obtains concessions and goes forward.
Just at present, one company alone holds a concession of
two thousand square miles in the interior. That means
mining rights ; and that means a few thousand coolies
and a settled administration such as obtains in the big
Indian collieries, where the heads of the mines are
responsible kings.

With the companies will come the railroads. So far
the Straits papers spend their space in talking about
them, for at present there are only twenty-three or
twenty-four miles of narrow-gauge railway open, near
a civilised place called Pirates' Creek, in the Peninsula. The Sultan of Johore is, or has been, wavering
over a concession for a railway through his country,
which will ultimately connect with this Pirates' Creek

line. Singapur is resolved ere long to bridge over the mile or mile-and-a-half Straits between herself and the State of Johore. In this manner a beginning will be made of the southerly extension of Colquhoun's great line running, let us say, from Singapur through the small States and Siam, without a break, into the great Indian railway systems, so that a man will be able to book from here to Calcutta direct. Anything like a business summary of the railway schemes that come up for discussion from time to time would fill a couple of these letters, and would be uncommonly dry reading. You know the sort of "shop" talk that rages among engineers when a new line is being run in India through perfectly known ground, whose traffic-potentialities may be calculated to the last pie. It is very much the same here, with the difference that no one knows for a certainty what the country ahead of the surveys is like, or where the development is likely to stop. This gives breeziness to the conversation. The audacity of the speakers is amazing to one who has been accustomed to see things through Indian eyes. They hint at "running up the Peninsula," establishing communications here, consolidating influence there, and Providence only knows what else ; but never a word do they breathe about the necessity for increased troops to stand by and back these little operations. Perhaps they assume that the Home Government will provide, but it does seem strange to hear them cold-bloodedly discussing notions that will inevitably demand doubled garrisons to keep the ventures out of alien hands. However, the merchant-men will do their work, and I suppose we shall borrow three files and a sergeant from somewhere or other when the time comes, and people begin to realise what sort of a gift our Straits Settlements are. It is so cheap to prophesy. They will in the near future grow into —

The Professor looked over my shoulder at this point. "Bosh!" said he. "They will become just a supplementary China — another field for Chinese cheap labour. When the Dutch Settlements were returned in 1815, — all these islands hereabouts, you know, — we should have handed over these places as well. Look!" He pointed at the swarming Chinamen below.

"Let me dream my dream, 'Fessor. I'll take my hat in a minute and settle the question of Chinese immigration in five minutes." But I confess it was mournful to look into the street, which ought to have been full of Beharis, Madrassis, and men from the Konkan — from our India.

Then up and spake a sunburned man who had interests in North Borneo — he owned caves in the mountains, some of them nine hundred feet high, so please you, and filled with the guano of ages, and had been telling me leech-stories till my flesh crawled. "North Borneo," said he, calmly, "wants a million of labourers to do her any good. One million coolies. Men are wanted everywhere, — in the Peninsula, in Sumatra for the tobacco planting, in Java, — everywhere; but Borneo — the Company's provinces that is to say — needs a million coolies." It is pleasant to oblige a stranger, and I felt that I spoke with India at my back. "We could oblige you with two million or twenty, for the matter of that," said I, generously.

"Your men are no good," said the North Borneo man.

"If one man goes away, he must have a whole village to look after his wants. India as a labour field is no good to us, and the Sumatra men say that your coolies either can't or won't tend tobacco properly. We must have China coolies as the land develops."

Oh, India, oh, my country! This it is to have inherited a highly organised civilisation and an ancient precedence code. That your children shall be scoffed at by the alien as useless outside their own pot-bound provinces. Here was a labour outlet, a door to full dinners, through which men — yellow men with pigtails — were pouring by the ten thousand, while in Bengal the cultured native editor was shrieking over "atrocities" committed in moving a few hundred souls a few hundred miles into Assam.

* * * * * * *

OF THE WELL-DRESSED ISLANDERS OF SINGAPUR AND
THEIR DIVERSIONS; PROVING THAT ALL STATIONS ARE
EXACTLY ALIKE. SHOWS HOW ONE CHICAGO JEW AND
AN AMERICAN CHILD CAN POISON THE PUREST MIND.

> "We are not divided,
> All one body we —
> One in hope and doctrine,
> One in Charity."

WHEN one comes to a new station the first thing to do
is to call on the inhabitants. This duty I had neglected,
preferring to consort with Chinese till the Sabbath,
when I learnt that Singapur went to the Botanical
Gardens and listened to secular music.

All the Englishmen in the island congregated there.
The Botanical Gardens would have been lovely at Kew,
but here, where one knew that they were the only place
of recreation open to the inhabitants, they were not
pleasant. All the plants of all the tropics grew there
together, and the orchid-house was roofed with thin
battens of wood — just enough to keep off the direct
rays of the sun. It held waxy-white splendours from
Manila, the Philippines, and tropical Africa — plants
that were half-slugs, drawing nourishment apparently
from their own wooden labels; but there was no
difference between the temperature of the orchid-house

and the open air; both were heavy, dank, and steaming.
I would have given a month's pay — but I have no
month's pay — for a clear breath of stifling hot wind
from the sands of Sirsa, for the darkness of a Punjab
dust-storm, in exchange for the perspiring plants, and
the tree-fern that sweated audibly.

Just when I was most impressed with my measureless
distance from India, my carriage advanced to the sound
of slow music, and I found myself in the middle of an
Indian station — not quite as big as Allahabad, and in-
finitely prettier than Lucknow. It overlooked the gardens that sloped in ridge and hollow below; and the
barracks were set in much greenery, and there was a
mess-house that suggested long and cooling drinks, and
there walked round about a British band. It was just
We Our Noble Selves. In the centre was the pretty
Memsahib with light hair and fascinating manners, and
the plump little *Memsahib* that talks to everybody and
is in everybody's confidence, and the spinster fresh from
home, and the bean-fed, well-groomed subaltern with the
light coat and fox-terrier. On the benches sat the fat
colonel, and the large judge, and the engineer's wife,
and the merchant-man and his family after their kind —
male and female met I them, and but for the little fact
that they were entire strangers to me, I would have
saluted them all as old friends. I knew what they
were talking about, could see them taking stock of one
another's dresses out of the corners of their eyes, could
see the young men backing and filling across the ground
in order to walk with the young maidens, and could
hear the "Do you think so's" and "Not really's" of
our polite conversation. It is an awful thing to sit in

a hired carriage and watch one's own people, and know
that though you know their life, you have neither part
nor lot in it.

> " I am a shadow now; alas! alas!
> Upon the skirts of human nature dwelling,"

I said mournfully to the Professor. He was looking at
Mrs. ——, or some one so like her that it came to the same
thing. "Am I travelling round the world to discover
these people?" said he. "I've seen 'em all before.
There's Captain Such-an-one and Colonel Such-another
and Miss What's-its-name as large as life and twice as
pale."

The Professor had hit it. That was the difference.
People in Singapur are dead-white — as white as Naaman
— and the veins on the backs of their hands are painted
in indigo.

It is as though the Rains were just over, and none of
the womenfolk had been allowed to go to the hills. Yet
no one talks about the unhealthiness of Singapur. A
man lives well and happily until he begins to feel un-
well. Then he feels worse because the climate allows
him no chance of pulling himself together — and then
he dies. Typhoid fever appears to be one gate of death,
as it is in India; also liver. The nicest thing in the civil
station which lies, of course, far from the native town,
and boasts pretty little bungalows — is Thomas — dear,
white-robed, swaggering, smoking, swearing Thomas Atkins the unchangeable, who listens to the band and
wanders down the bazaars, and slings the unmention-
able adjective about the palm trees exactly as though
he were in Mian Mir. The 58th (Northamptonshire)

live in these parts; so Singapur is quite safe, you see.

Nobody would speak to me in the gardens, though I felt that they ought to have invited me to drink, and I crept back to my hotel to eat six different fresh chutnies with one curry.

*　　*　　*　　*　　*　　*　　*

I want to go Home! I want to go back to India! I am miserable. The steamship *Nawab* at this time of the year ought to have been empty, instead of which we have one hundred first-class passengers and sixty-six second. All the pretty girls are in the latter class. Something must have happened at Colombo — two steamers must have clashed. We have the results of the collision, and we are a menagerie. The captain says that there ought to have been only ten or twelve passengers by rights, and had the rush been anticipated, a larger steamer would have been provided. Personally, I consider that half our shipmates ought to be thrown overboard. They are only travelling round the world for pleasure, and that sort of dissipation leads to the forming of hasty and intemperate opinions. Anyhow, give me freedom and the cockroaches of the British India, where we dined on deck, altered the hours of the meals by plebiscite, and were lords of all we saw. You know the chain-gang regulations of the P. and O.: how you must approach the captain standing on your head with your feet waving reverently; how you must crawl into the presence of the chief steward on your belly and call him Thrice-Puissant Bottle-washer; how you must not smoke abaft the sheep-pens; must not stand in the

companion; must put on a clean coat when the ship's
library is opened; and crowning injustice, must order
your drinks for tiffin and dinner one meal in advance?
How can a man full of Pilsener beer reach that keen-
set state of quiescence needful for ordering his dinner
liquor? This shows ignorance of human nature. The
P. and O. want healthy competition. They call their
captains commanders and act as though 'twere a favour
to allow you to embark. Again, freedom and the British
India for ever, and down with the comforts of a coolie
ship and the prices of a palace!

There are about thirty women on board, and I have
been watching with a certain amount of indignation their
concerted attempt at killing the stewardess, — a delicate
and sweet-mannered lady. I think they will accomplish
their end. The saloon is ninety feet long, and the stewardess runs up and down it for nine hours a day. In
her intervals of relaxation she carries cups of beef-tea to
the frail sylphs who cannot exist without food between
9 A.M. and 1 P.M. This morning she advanced to me and
said, as though it were the most natural thing in the
world: "Shall I take away your tea-cup, sir?" She
was a real white woman, and the saloon was full of
hulking, half-bred Portuguese. One young Englishman
let her take his cup, and actually did not turn round
when he handed it. This is awful, and teaches me, as
nothing else has done, how far I am from the blessed
East. She (the stewardess) talks standing up, to men
who sit down!

We in India are currently supposed to be unkind to
our servants. I should very much like to see a sweeper
doing one-half of the work these strapping white matrons

and maids exact from their sister. They make her carry things about and don't even say, "Thank you." She has no name, and if you bawl, "Stewardess," she is bound to come. Isn't it degrading?

But the real reason of my wish to return is because I have met a lump of Chicago Jews and am afraid that I shall meet many more. The ship is full of Americans, but the American-German-Jew boy is the most awful of all. One of them has money, and wanders from bow to stern asking strangers to drink, bossing lotteries on the run, and committing other atrocities. It is currently reported that he is dying. Unfortunately he does not die quickly enough.

But the real monstrosity of the ship is an American who is not quite grown up. I cannot call it a boy, though officially it is only eight, wears a striped jacket, and eats with the children. It has the wearied appearance of an infant monkey — there are lines round its mouth and under its eyebrows. When it has nothing else to do it will answer to the name of Albert. It has been two years on the continuous travel; has spent a month in India; has seen Constantinople, Tripoli, Spain; has lived in tents and on horseback for thirty days and thirty nights, as it was careful to inform me; and has exhausted the round of this world's delights. There is no flesh on its bones, and it lives in the smoking-room financing the arrangements of the daily lottery. I was afraid of it, but it followed me, and in a level expressionless voice began to tell me how lotteries were constructed. When I protested that I knew, it continued without regarding the interruption, and finally, as a reward for my patience, volunteered to give me the names and idiosyncrasies of all on board. Then it vanished through the smoking-room window because the door was only eight feet high, and therefore too narrow for that bulk of abnormal experiences. On certain subjects it was partly better informed than I; on others it displayed the infinite credulity of a two-year-old. But the wearied eyes were ever the same. They will be the same when it is fifty. I was more sorry for it than I could say. All its reminiscences had got jumbled, and incidents of Spain were baled into Turkey and India. Some day a schoolmaster will get hold of it and try to educate it, and I should dearly like to see at which end he will begin. The head is too full already and the — the other part does not exist. Albert is, I presume, but an ordinary American child. He was to me a revelation. Now I want to see a little American girl — but not now — not just now. My nerves are shattered by the Jews and Albert; and unless they recover their tone I shall turn back at Yokohama.

SHOWS HOW I ARRIVED IN CHINA AND SAW ENTIRELY
THROUGH THE GREAT WALL AND OUT UPON THE OTHER
SIDE.

> " Where naked ignorance
> Delivers brawling judgments all day long
> On all things unashamed."

THE past few days on the *Nawab* have been spent amid
a new people and a very strange one.   There were specu-
lators from South Africa: financiers from home (these
never talked in anything under hundreds of thousands of
pounds and, I fear, bluffed awfully) ; there were Consuls
of far-off China ports and partners of China shipping
houses talking a talk and thinking thoughts as different
from Ours as is Our slang from the slang of London.
But it would not interest you to learn the story of our
shipload — to hear about the hard-headed Scotch merchant with a taste for spiritualism, who begged me to tell
him whether there was really anything in Theosophy and
whether Tibet was full of levitating *chelas,* as he believed ;
or of the little London curate out for a holiday who had
seen India and had faith in the progress of missionary
work there — who believed that the C. M. S. was shaking
the thoughts and convictions of the masses, and that
the Word of the Lord would ere long prevail above all
other councils.   He in the night-watches tackled and dis

posed of the great mysteries of Life and Death, and was
looking forward to a lifetime of toil amid a parish without a single rich man in it.

When you are in the China Seas be careful to keep all
your flannel-wear to hand. In an hour the steamer
swung from tropical heat (including prickly) to a cold
raw fog, as wet as a Scotch mist. Morning gave us
a new world — somewhere between Heaven and Earth.
The sea was smoked glass: reddish grey islands lay
upon it under fog-banks that hovered fifty feet above
our heads. The squat sails of junks danced for an instant like autumn leaves in the breeze and disappeared,
and there was no solidity in the islands against which
the glassy levels splintered in snow. The steamer
groaned and grunted and howled because she was so
damp and miserable, and I groaned also because the
guide-book said that Hong-Kong had the finest harbour in the world, and I could not see two hundred
yards in any direction. Yet this ghost-like in-gliding
through the belted fog was livelily mysterious, and became more so when the movement of the air vouch-
safed us a glimpse of a warehouse and a derrick, both
apparently close aboard, and behind them the shoulder
of a mountain. We made our way into a sea of flat-
nosed boats all manned by most muscular humans,
and the Professor said that the time to study the Chinese question was now. We, however, were carrying a
new general to these parts, and nice, new, well-fitting
uniforms came off to make him welcome; and in the
contemplation of things too long withheld from me I
forgot about the Pigtails. Gentlemen of the mess-room,
who would wear linen coats on parade if you could,

wait till you have been a month without seeing a patrol-jacket or hearing a spur go *ling-a-ling,* and you will know why civilians want you always to wear uniform. The General, by the way, was a nice General. He did not know much about the Indian Army or the ways of a gentleman called Roberts, if I recollect aright; but he said that Lord Wolseley was going to be Commander-in-Chief one of these days on account of the pressing needs of our Army. He was a revelation because he talked about nothing but English military matters, which are very, very different from Indian ones, and are mixed up with politics.

All Hong-Kong is built on the sea face; the rest is fog. One muddy road runs for ever in front of a line of houses which are partly Chowringhee and partly Rotherhithe. You live in the houses, and when wearied of this, walk across the road and drop into the sea, if you can find a square foot of unencumbered water. So vast is the accumulation of country shipping, and such is its dirtiness as it rubs against the bund, that the superior inhabitants are compelled to hang their boats from davits above the common craft, who are greatly disturbed by a multitude of steam-launches. These ply for amusement and the pleasure of whistling, and are held in such small esteem that every hotel owns one, and the others are masterless. Beyond the launches lie more steamers than the eye can count, and four out of five of these belong to Us. I was proud when I saw the shipping at Singapur, but I swell with patriotism as I watch the fleets of Hong-Kong from the balcony of the Victoria Hotel. I can almost spit into the water; but many mariners stand below and they are a strong breed.

How recklessly selfish does a traveller become! We had dropped for more than ten days all the world outside our trunks, and almost the first word in the hotel was: "John Bright is dead, and there has been an awful hurricane at Samoa."

"Ah! indeed that's very sad; but look here, where do you say my rooms are?" At home the news would have given talk for half a day. It was dismissed in half the length of a hotel corridor. One cannot sit down to think with a new world humming outside the window — with all China to enter upon and possess.

A rattling of trunks in the halls — a click of heels — and the apparition of an enormous gaunt woman wrestling with a small Madrassi servant. . . . "Yes — I haf travelled everywhere and I shall travel everywhere else. I go now to Shanghai and Pekin. I have been in Moldavia, Russia, Beyrout, all Persia, Colombo, Delhi, Dacca, Benares, Allahabad, Peshawar, the Ali Musjid in that pass, Malabar, Singapur, Penang, here in this place, and Canton. I am Austrian-Croat, and I shall see the States of America and perhaps Ireland. I travel for ever; I am — how you call? — veuve — widow. My husband, he was dead; and so I am sad — I am always sad und so I trafel. I am alife of course, but I do not live. You onderstandt? Always sad. Vill you tell them the name of the ship to which they shall warf my trunks now. You trafel for pleasure? So! I trafel because I am alone und sad — always sad."

The trunks disappeared, the door shut, the heels clicked down the passage, and I was left scratching my head in wonder. How did that conversation begin — why did it end, and what is the use of meeting eccen-

tricities who never explained themselves? I shall never
get an answer, but that conversation is true, every word
of it. I see now where the fragmentary school of novelists get their material from.

When I went into the streets of Hong-Kong I stepped
into thick slushy London mud of the kind that strikes
chilly through the boot, and the rattle of innumerable
wheels was as the rattle of hansoms. A soaking rain
fell, and all the sahibs hailed 'rickshaws, — they call
them 'ricks here, — and the wind was chillier than the
rain. It was the first touch of honest weather since
Calcutta. No wonder with such a climate that Hong-
Kong was ten times livelier than Singapur, that there
were signs of building everywhere, and gas-jets in all
the houses, that colonnades and domes were scattered
broadcast, and the Englishmen walked as Englishmen
should — hurriedly and looking forward. All the length
of the main street was verandahed, and the Europe shops
squandered plate glass by the square yard. (*Nota bene.*
— As in Simla so elsewhere: mistrust the plate glass
shops. You pay for their fittings in each purchase.)

The same Providence that runs big rivers so near
to large cities puts main thoroughfares close to big
hotels. I went down Queen Street, which is not very
hilly. All the other streets that I looked up were built
in steps after the fashion of Clovelly, and under blue
skies would have given the Professor scores of good
photographs. The rain and the fog blotted the views
Each upward-climbing street ran out in white mist that
covered the sides of a hill, and the downward-sloping
ones were lost in the steam from the waters of the harbour, and both were very strange to see. " Hi-yi-yow,"

said my 'rickshaw coolie and balanced me on one wheel. I got out and met first a German with a beard, then three jolly sailor boys from a man-of-war, then a sergeant of Sappers, then a Parsee, then two Arabs, then an American, then a Jew, then a few thousand Chinese all carrying something, and then the Professor.

"They make plates — instantaneous plates — in Tokio, I'm told. What d' you think of that?" he said. "Why, in India, the Survey Department are the only people who make their own plates. Instantaneous plates in Tokio; think of it!"

I had owed the Professor one for a long time. "After all," I replied, "it strikes me that we have made the mistake of thinking too much of India. We thought we were civilised, for instance. Let us take a lower place. This beats Calcutta into a hamlet."

And in good truth it did, because it was clean beyond the ordinary, because the houses were uniform, three storied, and verandahed, and the pavements were of stone. I met one horse, very ashamed of himself, who was looking after a cart on the sea road, but upstairs there are no vehicles save 'rickshaws. Hong-Kong has killed the romance of the 'rickshaw in my mind. They ought to be sacred to pretty ladies, instead of which men go to office in them, officers in full canonicals use them; tars try to squeeze in two abreast, and from what I have heard down at the barracks they do occasionally bring to the guard-room the drunken defaulter. "He falls asleep inside of it, Sir, and saves trouble." The Chinese naturally have the town for their own, and profit by all our building improvements and regulations. Their golden and red signs flame down the Queen's Road,

but they are careful to supplement their own tongue
by well-executed Europe lettering. I found only one
exception, thus: —

> Fussing, Garpenter
> And Gabinet Naktr
> Has good Gabi
> Nets tor Sale.

The shops are made to catch the sailor and the curio
hunter, and they succeed admirably. When you come
to these parts put all your money in a bank and tell the
manager man not to give it you, however much you ask.
So shall you be saved from bankruptcy.

The Professor and I made a pilgrimage from Kee
Sing even unto Yi King, who sells the decomposed
fowl, and each shop was good. Though it sold shoes
or sucking pigs, there was some delicacy of carving
or gilded tracery in front to hold the eye, and each
thing was quaint and striking of its kind. A fragment
of twisted roots helped by a few strokes into the likeness of huddled devils, a running knop and flower
cornice, a dull red and gold half-door, a split bamboo
screen — they were all good, and their joinings and splic-
ings and mortisings were accurate. The baskets of the
coolies were good in shape, and the rattan fastenings
that clenched them to the polished bamboo yoke were
whipped down, so that there were no loose ends. You
could slide in and out the drawers in the slung chests
of the man who sold dinners to the 'rickshaw coolies;
and the pistons of the little wooden hand-pumps in the
shops worked accurately in their sockets.

I was studying these things while the Professor was
roaming through carved ivories, broidered silks, panels

of inlay, tortoise-shell filigree, jade-tipped pipes, and the God of Art only knows what else.

"I don't think even as much of him (meaning our Indian craftsman) as I used to do," said the Professor, taking up a tiny ivory grotesque of a small baby trying to pull a water-buffalo out of its wallow — the whole story of beast and baby written in the hard ivory. The same thought was in both our minds; we had gone near the subject once or twice before.

"They are a hundred times his superior in mere idea — let alone execution," said the Professor, his hand on a sketch in woods and gems of a woman caught in a gale of wind protecting her baby from its violence.

"Yes; and don't you see that *they* only introduce aniline dyes into things intended for *us*. Whereas *he* wears them on his body whenever he can. What made this yellow image of a shopman here take delight in a dwarf orange tree in a turquoise blue pot?" I continued, sorting a bundle of cheap China spoons — all good in form, colour, and use. The big-bellied Chinese lanterns above us swayed in the wind with a soft chafing of oiled paper, but they made no sign, and the shop-keeper in blue was equally useless.

"You wanchee buy? Heap plitty things here," said he; and he filled a tobacco-pipe from a dull green leather pouch held at the mouth with a little bracelet of plasma, or it might have been the very jade. He was playing with a brown-wood abacus, and by his side was his day-book bound in oiled paper, and the tray of Indian ink, with the brushes and the porcelain supports for the brushes. He made an entry in his book and daintily painted in his latest transaction. The

Chinese of course have been doing this for a few thousand years, but Life, and its experiences, is as new to me as it was to Adam, and I marvelled.

"Wanchee buy?" reiterated the shopman after he had made his last flourish.

"You," said I, in the new tongue which I am acquiring, "wanchee know one piecee information b'long my pidgin. Savvy these things? Have got soul, you?"

"Have got how?"

"Have got one piecee soul — allee same spilit? No savvy? This way then — your people lookee allee same devil; but makee culio allee same pocket-Joss, and not giving any explanation. Why-for are you such a horrible contradiction?"

"No savvy. Two dollar an' half," he said, balancing a cabinet in his hand. The Professor had not heard. His mind was oppressed with the fate of the Hindu.

"There are three races who can work," said the Professor, looking down the seething street where the 'rickshaws tore up the slush, and the babel of Cantonese, and pidgin went up to the yellow fog in a jumbled snarl.

"But there is only one that can swarm," I answered. "The Hindu cuts his own throat and dies, and there are too few of the Sahib-log to last for ever. These people work and spread. They must have souls or they couldn't understand pretty things."

"I can't make it out," said the Professor. "They are better artists than the Hindu, — that carving you are looking at is Japanese, by the way, — better artists and stronger workmen, man for man. They pack close and eat everything, and they can live on nothing."

"And I've been praising the beauties of Indian Art all

my days." It was a little disappointing when you come
to think of it, but I tried to console myself by the
thought that the two lay so far apart there was no com-
parison possible. And yet accuracy is surely the touch-
stone of all Art.

"They will overwhelm the world," said the Professor,
calmly, and he went out to buy tea.

Neither at Penang, Singapur, nor this place have
I seen a single Chinaman asleep while daylight lasted.
Nor have I seen twenty men who were obviously loafing.
All were going to some definite end — if it were only
like the coolie on the wharf, to steal wood from the
scaffolding of a half-built house. In his own land, I
believe, the Chinaman is treated with a certain amount
of carelessness, not to say ferocity. Where he hides his
love of art, the Heaven that made him out of the yellow earth that holds so much iron only knows. His
love is for little things, or else why should he get
quaint pendants for his pipe, and at the backmost back
of his shop build up for himself a bowerbird's collection
of odds and ends, every one of which has beauty if you
hold it sufficiently close to the eye. It grieves me that
I cannot account for the ideas of a few hundred million
men in a few hours. This much, however, seems certain. If we had control over as many Chinamen as we
have natives of India, and had given them one tithe
of the cossetting, the painful pushing forward, and
studious, even nervous, regard of their interests and
aspirations that we have given to India, we should long
ago have been expelled from, or have reaped the reward
of, the richest land on the face of the earth. A pair of
my shoes have been, oddly enough, wrapped in a news-

paper which carries for its motto the words, "There is no Indian nation, though there exists the germs of an Indian nationality," or something very like that. This thing has been moving me to unholy laughter. The great big lazy land that we nurse and wrap in cotton-wool, and ask every morning whether it is strong enough to get out of bed, seems like a heavy soft cloud on the far-away horizon; and the babble that we were wont to raise about its precious future and its possibilities, no more than the talk of children in the streets who have made a horse out of a pea-pod and match-sticks, and wonder if it will ever walk. I am sadly out of conceit of mine own other — not mother — country now that I have had my boots blacked at once every time I happened to take them off. The blacker did not do it for the sake of a gratuity, but because it was his work. Like the beaver of old, he had to climb that tree; the dogs were after him. There was competition.

* * * * * * *

Is there really such a place as Hong-Kong? People say so, but I have not yet seen it. Once indeed the clouds lifted and I saw a granite house perched like a cherub on nothing, a thousand feet above the town. It looked as if it might be the beginning of a civil station, but a man came up the street and said, "See this fog. It will be like this till September. You'd better go away." I shall not go. I shall encamp in front of the place until the fog lifts and the rain ceases. At present, and it is the third day of April, I am sitting in front of a large coal fire and thinking of the "frosty Caucasus" —you poor creatures in torment afar. And you think as you go to office and orderly-room that you are helping forward England's mission in the East. 'Tis a pretty delusion, and I am sorry to destroy it, but you have conquered the wrong country.

Let us annex China.

No. VIII

> "Love and let love, and so will I,
> But, sweet, for me no more with you,
> Not while I live, not though I die.
> Good night, good-by!"

I AM entirely the man about town, and sickness is no word for my sentiments. It began with an idle word in a bar-room. It ended goodness knows where. That the world should hold French, German, and Italian ladies of the ancient profession is no great marvel; but it is, to one who has lived in India, something shocking to meet again Englishwomen in the same sisterhood. When an opulent papa sends his son and heir round the world to enlarge his mind, does he reflect, I wonder, on the places into which the innocent strolls under the guidance of equally inexperienced friends? I am disposed to think that he does not. In the interest of the opulent papa, and from a genuine desire to see what they call Life, with a capital Hell, I went through Hong-Kong for the space of a night. I am glad that I am not a happy father with a stray son who thinks that he knows all the ropes. Vice must be pretty much the same all the round world over, but if a man wishes to get out of pleasure with it, let him go to Hong-Kong.

"Of course things are out and away better at 'Frisco," said my guide, "but we consider this very fair for the Island." It was not till a fat person in a black dressing-gown began to squeal demands for horrible stuff called "a bottle of wine" that I began to understand the glory of the situation. I was seeing Life. "Life" is a great thing. It consists in swigging sweet champagne that was stolen from a steward of the P. and O., and exchanging bad words with pale-faced baggages who laugh demnibly without effort and without emotion. The *argot* of the real "chippy" (this means man of the world — *Anglice*, a half-drunk youth with his hat on the back of his head) is not easy to come at. It requires an apprenticeship in America. I stood appalled at the depth and richness of the American language, of which I was privileged to hear a special dialect. There were girls who had been to Leadville and Denver and the wilds of the wilder West, who had acted in minor companies, and who had generally misconducted themselves in a hundred weary ways. They chattered like daws and shovelled down the sickly liquor that made the rooms reek. As long as they talked sensibly things were amusing, but a sufficiency of liquor made the mask drop, and verily they swore by all their gods, chief of whom is Obidicut. Very many men have heard a white woman swear, but some few, and among these I have been, are denied the experience. It is quite a revelation; and if nobody tilts you backwards out of your chair, you can reflect on heaps of

things connected with it. So they cursed and they drank
and they told tales, sitting in a circle, till I felt that
this was really Life and a thing to be quitted if I wished
to like it. The young man who knew a thing or two,
and gave the girls leave to sell him if they could, was
there of course, and the hussies sold him as he stood for
all he considered himself worth; and I saw the by-play.
Surely the safest way to be fooled is to know everything.
Then there was an interlude and some more shrieks and
howls, which the generous public took as indicating
immense mirth and enjoyment of Life; and I came to
yet another establishment, where the landlady lacked the
half of her left lung, as a cough betrayed, but was none
the less amusing in a dreary way, until she also dropped
the mask and the playful jesting began. All the jokes
I had heard before at the other place. It is a poor sort
of Life that cannot spring one new jest a day. More
than ever did the youth cock his hat and explain that he
was a real "chippy," and that there were no flies on him.
Any one without a cast-iron head would be "real chippy"
next morning after one glass of that sirupy champagne.
I understand now why men feel insulted when sweet fizz
is offered to them. The second interview closed as the
landlady gracefully coughed us into the passage, and so
into the healthy, silent streets. She was very ill indeed,
and announced that she had but four months more to live.

"Are we going to hold these dismal levees all through
the night ?" I demanded at the fourth house, where I
dreaded the repetition of the thrice-told tales.

"It's better in 'Frisco. Must amuse the girls a little
bit, y'know. Walk round and wake 'em up. That's
Life. You never saw it in India ?" was the reply.

"No, thank God, I didn't. A week of this would make me hang myself," I returned, leaning wearily against a door-post. There were very loud sounds of revelry by night here, and the inmates needed no waking up. One of them was recovering from a debauch of three days, and the other was just entering upon the same course. Providence protected me all through. A certain austere beauty of countenance had made every one take me for a doctor or a parson — a qualified parson, I think; and so I was spared many of the more pronounced jokes, and could sit and contemplate the Life that was so sweet. I thought of the Oxonian in *Tom and Jerry* playing jigs at the spinet, — you seen the old-fashioned plate, — while Corinthian Tom and Corinthian Kate danced a stately saraband in a little carpeted room. The worst of it was, the women were real women and pretty, and like some people I knew, and when they stopped the insensate racket for a while they were well behaved.

"Pass for real ladies anywhere," said my friend. "Aren't these things well managed?"

Then Corinthian Kate began to bellow for more drinks, — it was three in the morning, — and the current of hideous talk recommenced.

They spoke about themselves as "gay." This does not look much on paper. To appreciate the full grimness of the sarcasm hear it from their lips amid their own surroundings. I winked with vigour to show that I appreciated Life and was a real chippy, and that upon me, too, there were no flies. There is an intoxication in company that carries a man to excess of mirth; but when a party of four deliberately sit down to drink and swear, the bottom tumbles out of the amusement somehow, and loathing and boredom follow. A night's reflection has convinced me that there is no hell for these women in another world. They have their own in this Life, and I have been through it a little way. Still carrying the brevet rank of doctor, it was my duty to watch through the night to the dawn a patient — gay, *toujours* gay, remember — quivering on the verge of a complaint called the "jumps." Corinthian Kate will get hers later on. Her companion, emerging from a heavy drink, was more than enough for me. She was an unmitigated horror, until I lost detestation in genuine pity. The fear of death was upon her for a reason that you shall hear.

"I say, you say you come from India. Do you know anything about cholera?"

"A little," I answered. The voice of the questioner was cracked and quavering. A long pause.

"I say, Doctor, what are the symptoms of cholera? A woman died just over the street there last week."

"This is pleasant," I thought. "But I must remember that it is Life."

"She died last week — cholera. My God, I tell you she was dead in six hours! I guess I'll get cholera, too. I can't, though. Can I? I thought I had it two days ago. It hurt me terribly. I can't get it, can I? It never attacks people twice, does it? Oh, *say* it doesn't and be damned to you. Doctor, what are the symptoms of cholera?"

I waited till she had detailed her own attack, assured her that these and no others were the symptoms, and — may this be set to my credit — that cholera never

attacked twice. This soothed her for ten minutes
Then she sprang up with an oath and shrieked: —

"I won't be buried in Hong-Kong. That frightens me.
When I die — of cholera — take me to 'Frisco and bury
me there. In 'Frisco — Lone Mountain 'Frisco — you
hear, Doctor?"

I heard and promised. Outside the birds were beginning to twitter and the dawn was pencilling the shutters.

"I say, Doctor, did you ever know Cora Pearl?"

"'Knew *of* her." I wondered whether she was going
to walk round the room to all eternity with her eyes
glaring at the ceiling and her hands twisting and un-
twisting one within the other.

"Well," she began, in an impressive whisper, "it was
young Duval shot himself on her mat and made a bloody
mess there. I mean real bloody. You don't carry a
pistol, Doctor? Savile did. You didn't know Savile.
He was my husband in the States. But I'm English,
pure English. That's what I am. Let's have a bottle of
wine, I'm so nervous. Not good for me? What the —
No, you're a doctor. You know what's good against
cholera. Tell me! Tell me."

She crossed to the shutters and stared out, her hand
upon the bolt, and the bolt clacked against the wood
because of the tremulous hand.

"I tell you Corinthian Kate's drunk — full as she can
hold. She's always drinking. Did you ever see my
shoulder — these two marks on it? They were given
me by a man — a gentleman — the night before last. I
didn't fall against any furniture He struck me with
his cane twice, the beast, the beast, the beast! If I
had been full, I'd have knocked the dust out of him.

The beast! But I only went into the verandah and cried fit to break my heart. Oh, the beast!"

She paced the room, chafing her shoulder and crooning over it as though it were an animal. Then she swore at the man. Then she fell into a sort of stupor, but moaned and swore at the man in her sleep, and wailed for her *amah* to come and dress her shoulder.

Asleep she was not unlovely, but the mouth twitched and the body was shaken with shiverings, and there was no peace in her at all. Daylight showed her purple-eyed, slack-cheeked, and staring, racked with a headache and the nervous twitches. Indeed I was seeing Life; but it did not amuse me, for I felt that I, though I only made capital of her extreme woe, was guilty equally with the rest of my kind that had brought her here.

Then she told lies. At least I was informed that they were lies later on by the real man of the world. They related to herself and her people, and if untrue must have been motiveless, for all was sordid and sorrowful, though she tried to gild the page with a book of photos which linked her to her past. Not being a man of the world, I prefer to believe that the tales were true, and thank her for the honour she did me in the telling.

I had fancied that the house had nothing sadder to show me than her face. Here was I wrong. Corinthian Kate had really been drinking, and rose up reeling drunk, which is an awful thing to witness, and makes one's head ache sympathetically. Something had gone wrong in the slatternly menage where the plated tea-services were mixed with cheap China; and the household was being called to account. I watched her clutching the mosquito net for support, a horror and an offence in the eye of the guiltless day. I heard her swear in a thick, sodden voice as I have never yet heard a man swear, and I marvelled that the house did not thunder in on our heads. Her companion interposed, but was borne down by a torrent of blasphemy, and the half a dozen little dogs that infested the room removed themselves beyond reach of Corinthian Kate's hand or foot. That she was a handsome woman only made the matter worse. The companion collapsed shivering on one of the couches, and Kate swayed to and fro and cursed God and man and earth and heaven with puffed lips. If Alma Tadema could have painted her, — an arrangement in white, black hair, flashing eyes, and bare feet, — we should have seen the true likeness of the Eternal Priestess of Humanity. Or she would have been better drawn when the passion was over, tottering across the room, a champagne glass held high above her head, shouting, at ten o'clock in the morning, for some more of the infamous brewage that was even then poisoning the air of the whole house. She got her liquor, and the two women sat down to share it together. That was their breakfast.

I went away very sick and miserable, and as the door closed I saw the two drinking.

"Out and away better in 'Frisco," said the real "chippy" one. "But you see they are awfully nice — could pass for ladies any time they like. I tell you a man has to go round and keep his eyes open among them when he's seeing a little sporting life."

I have seen all that I wish to see, and henceforward I will pass. There may be better champagne and better drinkers in 'Frisco and elsewhere, but the talk will be the same, and the mouldiness and staleness of it all will be the same till the end of time. If this be Life, give me a little honest death, without drinks and without foul jesting. Anyway you look at it 'tis a poor performance, badly played, and too near to a tragedy to be pleasant. But it seems to amuse the young man wandering about the world, and I cannot believe that it is altogether good for him — unless, indeed, it makes him fonder of his home.

And mine was the greater sin! I was driven by no gust of passion, but went in cold blood to make my account of this Inferno, and to measure the measureless miseries of life. For the wholly insignificant sum of thirty dollars I had purchased information and disgust more than I required, and the right to look after a woman half crazed with drink and fear the third part of a terrible night. Mine was the greater sin.

When we stepped back into the world I was glad that the fog stood between myself and the heaven above.

No. IX

> "I should like to rise and go
> Where the golden apples grow,
> Where beneath another sky
> Parrot-islands anchored lie."
>
> — *R. L. Stevenson.*

HONG-KONG was so much alive, so built, so lighted, and so bloatedly rich to all outward appearance that I wanted to know how these things came about. You can't lavish granite by the cubic ton for nothing, or rivet your cliffs with Portland cement, or build a five-mile bund, or establish a club like a small palace. I sought a *Taipan*, which means the head of an English trading firm. He was the biggest *Taipan* on the island, and quite the nicest. He owned ships and wharves and houses and mines and a hundred other things. To him said I:—

"O *Taipan*, I am a poor person from Calcutta, and the liveliness of your place astounds me. How is it that every one smells of money; whence come your municipal improvements; and why are the White Men so restless?"

Said the *Taipan*: "It is because the island is going ahead mightily. Because everything pays. Observe this share-list."

He took me down a list of thirty or less companies — steam-launch companies, mining, rope-weaving, dock, trading, agency and general companies — and with five exceptions all the shares were at premium — some a hundred, some five hundred, and others only fifty.

"It is not a boom," said the *Taipan*. "It is genuine. Nearly every man you meet in these parts is a broker, and he floats companies."

I looked out of the window and beheld how companies were floated. Three men with their hats on the back of their heads converse for ten minutes. To these enters a fourth with a pocket-book. Then all four dive into the Hong-Kong Hotel for material wherewith to float themselves and — there is your company!

"From these things," said the *Taipan*, "comes the wealth of Hong-Kong. Every notion here pays, from the dairy-farm upwards. We have passed through our bad times and come to the fat years."

He told me tales of the old times — pityingly because he knew I could not understand. All I could tell was that the place dressed by America — from the hair-cutters' saloons to the liquor-bars. The faces of men were turned to the Golden Gate even while they floated most of the Singapur companies. There is not sufficient push in Singapur alone, so Hong-Kong helps. Circulars of new companies lay on the bank counters. I moved amid a maze of interests that I could not comprehend, and spoke to men whose minds were at Hankow, Foochoo, Amoy, or even further — beyond the Yangtze gorges where the Englishman trades.

After a while I escaped from the company-floaters because I knew I could not understand them, and ran

up a hill. Hong-Kong is all hill except when the fog
shuts out everything except the sea. Tree ferns sprouted
on the ground and azaleas mixed with the ferns, and
there were bamboos over all. Consequently it was only
natural that I should find a tramway that stood on its
head and waved its feet in the mist. They called it the
Victoria Gap Tramway and hauled it up with a rope. It
ran up a hill into space at an angle of 65°, and to those
who have seen the Rigi, Mount Washington, a switch-
back railway, and the like would not have been impressive. But neither you nor I have ever been hauled
from Annandale to the Chaura Maidàn in a bee-line
with a five-hundred-foot drop on the off-side, and we
are at liberty to marvel. It is not proper to run up
inclined ways at the tail of a string, more especially
when you cannot see two yards in front of you and all
earth below is a swirling cauldron of mist. Nor, unless
you are warned of the opticalness of the delusion, is it
nice to see from your seat, houses and trees at magic-
lantern angles. Such things, before tiffin, are worse
than the long roll of the China seas.

They turned me out twelve hundred feet above the
city on the military road to Dalhousie, as it will be when
India has a surplus. Then they brought me a glorified
dandy which, not knowing any better, they called a chair.
Except that it is too long to run corners easily, a chair is
vastly superior to a dandy. It is more like a Bombay
side *tonjon* — the kind we use at Mahableshwar. You sit
in a wicker chair, slung low on ten feet of elastic wooden
shafting, and there are light blinds against the rain.

"We are now," said the Professor, as he wrung out his
hat gemmed with the dews of the driving mist, "we are

now on a pleasure trip. This is the road to Chakrata in the rains."

"Nay," said I; "it is from Solon to Kasauli that we are going. Look at the black rocks."

"Bosh!" said the Professor. "This is a civilised country. Look at the road, look at the railings — look at the gutters."

And as I hope never to go to Solon again, the road was cemented, the railings were of iron mortised into granite blocks, and the gutters were paved. 'Twas no wider than a hill-path, but if it had been the Viceroy's pet promenade it could not have been better kept. There was no view. That was why the Professor had taken his camera. We passed coolies widening the road, and houses shut up and deserted, solid squat little houses made of stone, with pretty names after our hill-station custom — Townend, Craggylands, and the like — and at these things my heart burned within me. Hong-Kong has no right to mix itself up with Mussoorie in this fashion. We came to the meeting-place of the winds, eighteen hundred feet above all the world, and saw forty miles of clouds. That was the Peak — the great view-place of the island. A laundry on a washing day would have been more interesting.

"Let us go down, Professor," said I, "and we'll get our money back. This isn't a view."

We descended by the marvellous tramway, each pretending to be as little upset as the other, and started in pursuit of a Chinese burying-ground.

"Go to the Happy Valley," said an expert. "The Happy Valley, where the racecourse and the cemeteries are."

"It's Mussoorie," said the Professor. "I knew it all along."

It was Mussoorie, though we had to go through a half-mile of Portsmouth Hard first. Soldiers grinned at us from the verandahs of their most solid three-storied barracks; all the blue-jackets of all the China squadron were congregated in the Royal Navy Seaman's Club, and they beamed upon us. The blue-jacket is a beautiful creature, and very healthy, but . . . I gave my heart to Thomas Atkins long ago, and him I love.

By the way, how is it that a Highland regiment — the Argyll and Southerlandshire for instance — get such good recruits? Do the kilt and sporran bring in brawny youngsters of five-foot nine, and thirty-nine inch round the chest? The Navy draws well-built men also. How is it that Our infantry regiments fare so badly?

We came to the Happy Valley by way of a monument to certain dead Englishmen. Such things cease to move emotion after a little while. They are but the seed of the great harvest whereof our children's children shall assuredly reap the fruits. The men were killed in a fight, or by disease. We hold Hong-Kong, and by Our strength and wisdom it is a great city, built upon a rock, and furnished with a dear little seven-furlong racecourse set in the hills, and fringed as to one side with the homes of the dead — Mahometan, Christian, and Parsee. A wall of bamboos shuts off the course and the grand-stand from the cemeteries. It may be good enough for Hong-Kong, but would you care to watch your pony running with a grim reminder of "gone to the drawer" not fifty feet behind you? Very beautiful are the cemeteries, and very carefully tended. The rocky hillside rises so near to them that the more recent dead can almost command a view of the racing as they lie. Even this far from the strife of the Churches they bury the different sects of Christians apart. One creed paints its wall white, and the other blue. The latter, as close to the race-stand as may be, writes in straggling letters, "*Hodie mihi cras tibi.*" No, I should *not* care to race in Hong-Kong. The scornful assemblage behind the grand-stand would be enough to ruin any luck.

Chinamen do not approve of showing their cemeteries. We hunted ours from ledge to ledge of the hillsides, through crops and woods and crops again, till we came to a village of black and white pigs and riven red rocks beyond which the dead lay. It was a third-rate place, but was pretty. I have studied that oilskin mystery, the Chinaman, for at least five days, and why he should elect to be buried in good scenery, and by what means he knows good scenery when he sees it, I cannot fathom. But he gets it when the sight is taken from him, and his friends fire crackers above him in token of the triumph.

That night I dined with the *Taipan* in a palace. They say the merchant prince of Calcutta is dead — killed by exchange. Hong-Kong ought to be able to supply one or two samples. The funny thing in the midst of all this wealth — wealth such as one reads about in novels — is to hear the curious deference that is paid to Calcutta. Console yourselves with that, gentlemen of the Ditch, for by my faith, it is the one thing that you can boast of. At this dinner I learned that Hong-Kong was impregnable and that China was rapidly importing twelve and forty ton guns for the defence of her coasts. The one statement I doubted, but the other was truth. Those who have occasion to speak of China in these parts do so deferentially, as who should say: " Germany intends such and such," or " These are the views of Russia." The very men who talk thus are doing their best to force upon the great Empire all the stimulants of the West-railways, tram lines, and so forth. What will happen when China really wakes up, runs a line from Shanghai to Lhassa, starts another line of imperial Yellow Flag immigrant steamers, and really works and controls her own gun-factories and arsenals? The energetic Englishmen who ship the forty-tonners are helping to this end, but all they say is: " We're well paid for what we do. There's no sentiment in business, and anyhow, China will never go to war with England." Indeed, there is no sentiment in business. The *Taipan's* palace, full of all things beautiful, and flowers more lovely than the gem-like cabinets they adorned, would have made happy half a hundred young men craving for luxury, and might have made them writers, singers, and poets. It was inhabited by men with big heads and straight eyes, who sat among the splendours and talked business.

If I were not going to be a Burman when I die I would be a *Taipan* at Hong-Kong. He knows so much and he deals so largely with Princes and Powers, and he has a flag of his very own which he pins on to all his steamers.

The blessed chance that looks after travellers sent me next day on a picnic, and all because I happened to wander into the wrong house. This is quite true, and very like our Anglo-Indian ways of doing things.

"Perhaps," said the hostess, "this will be our only fine day. Let us spend it in a steam-launch."

Forthwith we embarked upon a new world — that of Hong-Kong harbour — and with a dramatic regard for the fitness of things our little ship was the *Pioneer*. The picnic included the new General — he that came from England in the *Nawab* and told me about Lord Wolseley — and his aide-de-camp, who was quite English and altogether different from an Indian officer. He never once talked shop, and if he had a grievance hid it behind his mustache.

The harbour is a great world in itself. Photographs say that it is lovely, and this I can believe from the glimpses caught through the mist as the *Pioneer* worked her way between the lines of junks, the tethered liners, the wallowing coal hulks, the trim, low-lying American corvette, the *Orontes*, huge and ugly, the *Cockchafer*, almost as small as its namesake, the ancient three-decker converted into a military hospital, — Thomas gets change of air thus, — and a few hundred thousand sampans manned by women with babies tied on to their backs. Then we swept down the sea face of the city and saw that it was great, till we came to an unfinished fort high up on the side of a green hill, and I watched the new General as men watch an oracle. Have I told you that he is an Engineer General, specially sent out to attend to the fortifications? He looked at the raw earth and the granite masonry, and there was keen professional interest in his eye. Perhaps he would say something. I edged nearer in that hope. He did: —

"Sherry and sandwiches? Thanks, I will. 'Stonishing how hungry the sea-air makes a man feel," quoth the

General; and we went along under the grey-green coast, looking at stately country houses made of granite, where Jesuit fathers and opulent merchants dwell. It was the Mashobra of this Simla. It was also the Highlands, it was also Devonshire, and it was specially grey and chilly.

Never did *Pioneer* circulate in stranger waters. On the one side was a bewildering multiplicity of islets; on the other, the deeply indented shores of the main island, sometimes running down to the sea in little sandy coves, at others falling sheer in cliff and sea-worn cave full of the boom of the breakers. Behind, rose the hills into the mist, the everlasting mist.

"We are going to Aberdeen," said the hostess; "then to Stanley, and then across the island on foot by way of the Ti-tam reservoir. That will show you a lot of the country."

We shot into a fiord and discovered a brown fishing village which kept sentry over two docks, and a Sikh policeman. All the inhabitants were rosy-cheeked women, each owning one-third of a boat, and a whole baby, wrapped up in red cloth and tied to the back. The mother was dressed in blue for a reason, — if her husband whacked her over the shoulders, he would run a fair chance of crushing the baby's head unless the infant were of a distinct colour.

Then we left China altogether, and steamed into far Lochaber, with a climate to correspond. Good people under the punkah, think for a moment of cloud-veiled headlands running out into a steel-grey sea, crisped with a cheek-rasping breeze that makes you sit down under the bulwarks and gasp for breath. Think of the merry pitch and roll of a small craft as it buzzes from island to island, or venturously cuts across the mouth of a mile-wide bay, while you mature amid fresh scenery, fresh talk, and fresh faces, an appetite that shall uphold the credit of the great empire in a strange land. Once more we found a village which they called Stanley; but it was different from Aberdeen. Tenantless buildings of brown-stone stared seaward from the low downs, and there lay behind them a stretch of weather-beaten wall. No need to ask what these things meant. They cried aloud: "It is a deserted cantonment, and the population is in the cemetery."

"I asked, "What regiment?"

"The Ninety-second, I think," said the General. "But that was in the old times — in the Sixties. I believe they quartered a lot of troops here and built the bar-racks on the ground; and the fever carried all the men off like flies. Isn't it a desolate place?"

My mind went back to a neglected graveyard a stone's throw from Jehangir's tomb in the gardens of Shalimar, where the cattle and the cowherd look after the last resting-places of the troops who first occupied Lahore. We are a great people and very strong, but we build Our empire in a wasteful manner — on the bones of the dead that have died of disease.

"But about the fortifications, General? Is it true that etc., etc.?"

"The fortifications are right enough as things go; what we want is men."

"How many?"

"Say about three thousand for the Island — enough to stop any expedition that might come. Look at all these little bays and coves. There are twenty places at the back of the island where you could land men and make things unpleasant for Hong-Kong."

"But," I ventured, "isn't it the theory that any organised expedition ought to be stopped by our fleet before it got here? Whereas the forts are supposed to prevent cutting out, shelling, and ransoming by a disconnected man-of-war or two."

"If you go on that theory," said the General, "the men-of-war ought to be stopped by our fleets, too. That's all nonsense. If any Power can throw troops here, you want troops to turn 'em out, and — don't we wish we may get them!"

"And you? Your command here is for five years, isn't it?"

"Oh, no! Eighteen months ought to see me out. I don't want to stick here for ever. I've other notions for myself," said the General, scrambling over the boulders to get at his tiffin.

And that is just the worst of it. Here was a nice General helping to lay out fortifications, with one eye on Hong-Kong and the other, his right one, on England. He would be more than human not to sell himself and his orders for the command of a brigade in the next English affair. He would be afraid of being too long away from home lest he should drop out of the running and . . . Well, we are just the same in India, and there is not the least hope of raising a Legion of the Lost for colonial service — of men who would do their work in one place for ever and look for nothing beyond it. But remember that Hong-Kong — with five million tons of coal, five miles of shipping, docks, wharves, huge civil

station, forty million pounds of trade, and the nicest
picnic parties that you ever did see — wants three thousand men and — she won't get them. She has two bat-
teries of garrison artillery, a regiment, and a lot of
gun lascars — about enough to prevent the guns from
rusting on their carriages. There are three forts on
an island — Stonecutter's Island — between Hong-Kong
and the mainland, three on Hong-Kong itself, and three
or four scattered about elsewhere. Naturally the full
complement of guns has not arrived. Even in India you
cannot man forts without trained gunners. But tiffin
under the lee of a rock was more interesting than colonial defence. A man cannot talk politics if he be empty.

Our one fine day shut in upon the empty plates in
wind and rain, and the march across the island began.

As the launch was blotted out in the haze we squelched
past sugar-cane crops and fat pigs, past the bleak cemetery of dead soldiers on the hill, across a section of
moor, till we struck a hill-road above the sea. The
views shifted and changed like a kaleidoscope. First
a shaggy shoulder of land tufted with dripping rushes
and naught above, beneath, or around but mist and
the straight spikes of the rain; then red road swept
by water that fell into the unknown; then a combe,
straight walled almost as a horse, at the bottom of which
crawled the jade-green sea; then a vista of a bay, a bank
of white sand, and a red-sailed junk beating out before
the squall; then only wet rock and fern, and the voice
of thunder calling from peak to peak.

A landward turn in the road brought us to the pine
woods of Theog and the rhododendrons — but they called
them azaleas — of Simla, and ever the rain fell as though

it had been July in the hills instead of April at Hong
Kong.   An invading army marching upon Victoria would
have a sad time of it even if the rain did not fall.   There
are but one or two gaps in the hills through which it
could travel, and there is a scheme in preparation whereby
they shall be cut off and annihilated when they come.
When I had to climb a clay hill backwards digging my
heels into the dirt, I very much pitied that invading
army.

Whether the granite-faced reservoir and two-mile tunnel that supplies Hong-Kong with water be worth seeing
I cannot tell.   There was too much water in the air for
comfort even when one tried to think of Home.

But go you and take the same walk — ten miles, and
only two of 'em on level ground.   Steam to the forsaken
cantonment of Stanley and cross the island, and tell me
whether you have seen anything so wild and wonderful
in its way as the scenery.   I am going up the river to
Canton, and cannot stay for word-paintings.

SHOWS HOW I CAME TO GOBLIN MARKET AND TOOK A
SCUNNER AT IT AND CURSED THE CHINESE PEOPLE.
SHOWS FURTHER HOW I INITIATED ALL HONG-KONG
INTO OUR FRATERNITY.

PROVIDENCE is pleased to be sarcastic. It sent rain
and a raw wind from the beginning till the end. That is
one of the disadvantages of leaving India. You cut yourself adrift from the only trustworthy climate in the
world. I despise a land that has to waste half its
time in watching the clouds. The Canton trip (I have
been that way) introduces you to the American river
steamer, which is not in the least like one of the
Irrawaddy flotilla or an omnibus, as many people believe. It is composed almost entirely of white paint,
sheet-lead, a cow-horn, and a walking-beam, and holds
about as much cargo as a P. and O. The trade between
Canton and Hong-Kong seems to be immense, and a
steamer covers the ninety miles between port and port
daily. None the less are the Chinese passengers daily
put under hatches or its equivalent after they leave port,
and daily is the stand of loaded Sniders in the cabin
inspected and cleaned up. Daily, too, I should imagine,
the captain of each boat tells his Globe-trotting passengers
the venerable story of the looting of a river steamer —
how two junks fouled her at a convenient bend in the

river, while the native passengers on her rose and made things very lively for the crew, and ended by clearing out that steamer. The Chinese are a strange people! They had a difficulty at Hong-Kong not very long ago about photographing labour coolies, and in the excitement, which was considerable, a rickety old war junk got into position off the bund with the avowed intention of putting a three-pound shot through the windows of the firm who had suggested the photographing. And this though vessel and crew could have been blown in cigarette-ash in ten minutes!

But no one pirated the *Ho-nam*, though the passengers did their best to set her on fire by upsetting the lamps of their opium pipes. She blared her unwieldy way across the packed shipping of the harbour and ran into grey mist and driving rain. When I say that the scenery was like the West Highlands you will by this time understand what I mean. Large screw steamers, China pig-boats very low in the water and choked with live-stock, wallowing junks and ducking sampans filled the waterways of a stream as broad as the Hughli and much better defended so far as the art of man was concerned. Their little difficulty with the French a few years ago has taught the Chinese a great many things which, perhaps, it were better for us that they had left alone.

The first striking object of Canton city is the double tower of the big Catholic Church. Take off your hat to this because it means a great deal, and stands as the visible standard of a battle that has yet to be fought. Never have the missionaries of the Mother of the Churches wrestled so mightily with any land as with China, and never has nation so scientifically tortured the mis-

sionary as has China. Perhaps when the books are
audited somewhere else, each race, the White and the
Yellow, will be found to have been right according to
their lights.

I had taken one fair look at the city from the steamer,
and threw up my cards. "I can't describe this place,
and besides, I hate Chinamen."

"Bosh! It is only Benares, magnified about eight
times. Come along."

It was Benares, without any wide streets or chauks,
and yet darker than Benares, in that the little skyline
was entirely blocked by tier on tier of hanging signs, —
red, gold, black, and white. The shops stood on granite
plinths, pukka brick above, and tile-roofed. Their fronts
were carved wood, gilt, and coloured savagely. John
knows how to dress a shop, though he may sell nothing
more lovely than smashed fowl and chitterlings. Every
other shop was a restaurant, and the space between
them crammed with humanity. Do you know those
horrible sponges full of worms that grow in warm
seas? You break off a piece of it and the worms break
too. Canton was that sponge. "Hi, low yah. To hoh
wang!" yelled the chair-bearers to the crowd, but I was
afraid that if the poles chipped the corner of a house the
very bricks would begin to bleed. Hong-Kong showed
me how the Chinaman could work. Canton explained why
he set no value on life. The article was cheaper than
in India. I hated the Chinaman before; I hated him
doubly as I choked for breath in his seething streets
where nothing short of the pestilence could clear a
way. There was of course no incivility from the people,
but the mere mob was terrifying. There are three

or four places in the world where it is best for an Eng
lishman to agree with his adversary swiftly, whatever
the latter's nationality may be. Canton heads the list.
Never argue with anybody in Canton. Let the guide do
it for you. Then the stinks rose up and overwhelmed
us. In this respect Canton was Benares twenty times
magnified. The Hindu is a sanitating saint compared
to the Chinaman. He is a rigid Malthusian in the
same regard.

"Very bad stink, this place. You come right along,"
said Ah Cum, who had learned his English from Americans. He was very kind. He showed me feather-jewellery
shops where men sat pinching from the gorgeous wings of
jays, tiny squares of blue and lilac feathers, and pasting
them into gold settings, so that the whole looked like
Jeypore enamel of the rarest. But we went into a shop.
Ah Cum drew us inside the big door and bolted it, while
the crowd blocked up the windows and shutter-bars. I
thought more of the crowd than the jewellery. The city
was so dark and the people were so very many and so
unhuman.

The March of the Mongol is a pretty thing to write
about in magazines. Hear it once in the gloom of an
ancient curio shop, where nameless devils of the Chinese
creed make mouths at you from back-shelves, where
brazen dragons, revelations of uncleanliness, all catch
your feet as you stumble across the floor — hear the
tramp of the feet on the granite blocks of the road and
the breaking wave of human speech, that is not human!
Watch the yellow faces that glare at you between the
bars, and you will be afraid, as I was afraid.

"It's beautiful work," said the Professor, bending over

a Cantonese petticoat — a wonder of pale green, blue, and silver. " Now I understand why the civilised European of Irish extraction kills the Chinaman in America. It is justifiable to kill him. It would be quite right to wipe the city of Canton off the face of the earth, and to exterminate all the people who ran away from the shelling. The Chinaman ought not to count."

I had gone off on my own train of thought, and it was a black and bitter one.

" Why on earth can't you look at the lions and enjoy yourself, and leave politics to the men who pretend to understand 'em ? " said the Professor.

"It's no question of politics," I replied. " This people ought to be killed off because they are unlike any people I ever met before. Look at their faces. They despise us. You can see it, and they aren't a bit afraid of us either."

Then Ah Cum took us by ways that were dark to the temple of the Five Hundred Genii, which was one of the sights of the rabbit-warren. This was a Buddhist temple with the usual accessories of altars and altar lights and colossal figures of doorkeepers at the gates. Round the inner court runs a corridor lined on both sides with figures about half life-size, representing most of the races of Asia. Several of the Jesuit Fathers are said to be in that gallery, — you can find it all in the guide-books, — and there is one image of a jolly-looking soul in a hat and full beard, but, like the others, naked to the waist. " That European gentleman," said Ah Cum. " That Marco Polo." " Make the most of him," I said. " The time is coming when there will be no European gentlemen — nothing but yellow people with black hearts

— black hearts, Ah Cum — and a devil-born capacity for doing more work than they ought."

"Come and see a clock," said he. "Old clock. It runs by water. Come on right along." He took us to another temple and showed us an old water-clock of four *gurrahs:* just the same sort of thing as they have in out-of-the-way parts of India for the use of the watchmen. The Professor vows that the machine, which is supposed to give the time to the city, is regulated by the bells of the steamers in the river, Canton water being too thick to run through anything smaller than a half-inch pipe. From the pagoda of this temple we could see that the roofs of all the houses below were covered with filled water-jars. There is no sort of fire organisation in the city. When lighted it burns till it stops.

Ah Cum led us to the Potter's Field, where the executions take place. The Chinese slay by the hundred, and far be it from me to say that such generosity of blood-shed is cruel. They could afford to execute in Canton alone at the rate of ten thousand a year without disturbing the steady flow of population. An executioner who happened to be wandering about — perhaps in search of employment — offered us a sword under guarantee that it had cut off many heads. "Keep it," I said. "Keep it, and let the good work go on. My friend, you cannot execute too freely in this land. You are blessed, I apprehend, with a purely literary bureaucracy recruited — correct me if I am wrong — from all social strata, more especially those in which the idea of cold-blooded cruelty has, as it were, become embedded. Now, when to inherited devildom is superadded a purely literary education of grim and formal tendencies, the result my evil-looking friend, — the result, I repeat, — is a state of affairs which is faintly indicated in the Little Pilgrim's account of the Hell of Selfishness. You, I presume, have not yet read the works of the Little Pilgrim."

" He looks as if he was going to cut at you with that sword," said the Professor. " Come away and see the Temple of Horrors."

That was a sort of Chinese Madame Tussaud's — life-like models of men being brayed in mortars, sliced, fried, toasted, stuffed, and variously bedevilled — that made me sick and unhappy. But the Chinese are merciful even in their tortures. When a man is ground in a mill, he is, according to the models, popped in head first. This is hard on the crowd who are waiting to see the fun, but it saves trouble to the executioners. A half-ground man has to be carefully watched, or else he wriggles out of his place. To crown all, we went to the prison, which was a pest-house in a back street. The Professor shuddered. " It's all right," I said. " The people who sent the prisoners here don't care. The men themselves look hideously miserable, but I suppose they don't care, and goodness knows I don't care. They are only Chinamen. If they treat each other like dogs, why should we regard 'em as human beings? Let 'em rot. I want to get back to the steamer. I want to get under the guns of Hong-Kong. Phew!"

Then we ran through a succession of second-rate streets and houses till we reached the city wall on the west by a long flight of steps. It was clean here. The wall had a drop of thirty or forty feet to paddy fields. Beyond these were a semicircle of hills, every square

yard of which is planted out with graves. Her dead
watch Canton the abominable, and the dead are more
than the myriads living. On the grass-grown top of the
wall were rusty English guns spiked and abandoned after
the war. They ought not to be there. A five-storied
pagoda gave us a view of the city, but I was wearied of
these rats in their pit — wearied and scared and sullen.
The excellent Ah Cum led us to the Viceroy's summer
garden-house on the cityward slope of an azalea-
covered hill surrounded by cotton trees. The basement
was a handsome joss house: upstairs was a durbar-hall
with glazed verandahs and ebony furniture ranged across
the room in four straight lines. It was only an oasis of
cleanliness. Ten minutes later we were back in the
swarming city, cut off from light and sweet air. Once
or twice we met a mandarin with thin official mustache and "little red button a-top." Ah Cum was explaining the nature and properties of a mandarin when
we came to a canal spanned by an English bridge and
closed by an iron gate, which was in charge of a Hong-
Kong policeman. We were in an Indian station with
Europe shops and Parsee shops and everything else to
match. This was English Canton, with two hundred
and fifty sahibs in it. 'Twould have been better for a
Gatling behind the bridge gate. The guide-books tell
you that it was taken from the Chinese by the treaty of
1860, the French getting a similar slice of territory.
Owing to the binding power of French officialism, "La
concession Française" has never been let or sold to
private individuals, and now a Chinese regiment squats
on it. The men who travel tell you somewhat similar
tales about land in Saigon and Cambodia. Something

seems to attack a Frenchman as soon as he dons a colonial uniform. Let us call it the red-tape-worm.

"Now where did you go and what did you see?" said the Professor, in the style of the pedagogue, when we were once more on the *Ho-nam* and returning as fast as steam could carry us to Hong-Kong.

"A big blue sink of a city full of tunnels, all dark and inhabited by yellow devils, a city that Doré ought to have seen. I'm devoutly thankful that I'm never going back there. The Mongol will begin to march in his own good time. I intend to wait until he marches up to me. Let us go away to Japan by the next boat."

The Professor says that I have completely spoiled the foregoing account by what he calls "intemperate libels on a hard-working nation." He did not see Canton as I saw it — through the medium of a fevered imagination.

Once, before I got away, I climbed to the civil station of Hong-Kong, which overlooks the town. There in sumptuous stone villas built on the edge of the cliff and facing shaded roads, in a wilderness of beautiful flowers and a hushed calm unvexed even by the roar of the traffic below, the residents do their best to imitate the life of an India up-country station. They are better off than we are. At the bandstand the ladies dress all in one piece — shoes, gloves, and umbrellas come out from England with the dress, and every *memsahib* knows what that means — but the mechanism of their life is much the same. In one point they are superior. The ladies have a club of their very own to which, I believe, men are only allowed to come on sufferance. At a dance there are about twenty men to one lady, and there are practically no spinsters in the island. The inhabitants complain

of being cooped in and shut up. They look at the sea
below them and they long to get away. They have their
" At Homes " on regular days of the week, and everybody meets everybody else again and again. They have
amateur theatricals and they quarrel and all the men and
women take sides, and the station is cleaved asunder from
the top to the bottom. Then they become reconciled and
write to the local papers condemning the local critic's
criticism. Isn't it touching? A lady told me these
things one afternoon, and I nearly wept from sheer
home-sickness.

"And then, you know, after she had said *that* he was
obliged to give the part to the other, and that made *them*
furious, and the races were so near that nothing could be
done, and Mrs. —— said that it was altogether impossible. You understand how very unpleasant it must have
been, do you not ? "

"Madam," said I, "I do. I have been there before.
My heart goes out to Hong-Kong. In the name of the
great Indian Mofussil I salute you. Henceforward
Hong-Kong is one of Us, ranking before Meerut, but after
Allahabad, at all public ceremonies and parades."

I think she fancied I had sunstroke ; but you at any
rate will known what I mean.

We do not laugh any more on the P. and O. S. S.
Ancona on the way to Japan. We are deathly sick,
because there is a cross-sea beneath us and a wet sail
above. The sail is to steady the ship who refuses to be
steadied. She is full of Globe-trotters who also refuse to
be steadied. A Globe-trotter is extreme cosmopolitan.
He will be sick anywhere.

No. XI

> "Thou canst not wave thy staff in air
> Or dip thy paddle in the lake,
> But it carves the bow of beauty there,
> And ripples in rhyme the oar forsake."— *Emerson.*

THIS morning, after the sorrows of the rolling night, my cabin porthole showed me two great grey rocks studded and streaked with green and crowned by two stunted blue-black pines. Below the rocks a boat, that might have been carved sandal wood for colour and delicacy, was shaking out an ivory-white frilled sail to the wind of the morning. An indigo-blue boy with an old ivory face hauled on a rope. Rock and tree and boat made a panel from a Japanese screen, and I saw that the land was not a lie. This "good brown earth" of ours has many pleasures to offer her children, but there be few in her gift comparable to the joy of touching a new coun-try, a completely strange race, and manners contrary. Though libraries may have been written aforetime, each new beholder is to himself another Cortez. And I was in Japan — the Japan of cabinets and joinery gracious folk and fair manners. Japan, whence the camphor and the lacquer and the shark-skin swords come : among what was it the books said ? — a nation of artists. To be sure, we should only stop at Nagasaki for twelve hours ere going on to Kobé, but in twelve hours one can pack away a very fair collection of new experiences.

An execrable man met me on the deck, with a pale-blue pamphlet fifty pages thick. " Have you," said he, " seen the Constitution of Japan ? The Emperor made it him- self only the other day. It is on entirely European lines."

I took the pamphlet and found a complete paper Con- stitution stamped with the Imperial Chrysanthemum — an excellent little scheme of representation, reforms, payment of members, budget estimates, and legislation. It is a terrible thing to study at close quarters, because it is so pitifully English.

There was a yellow-shot greenness upon the hills round Nagasaki different, so my willing mind was dis- posed to believe, from the green of other lands. It was the green of a Japanese screen, and the pines were screen pines. The city itself hardly showed from the crowded harbour. It lay low among the hills, and its business face — a grimy bund — was sloppy and deserted. Busi- ness, I was rejoiced to learn, was at a low ebb in Nagasaki. The Japanese should have no concern with business. Close to one of the still wharves lay a ship of the Bad People; a Russian steamer down from Vladi- vostok. Her decks were cumbered with raffle of all kinds; her rigging was as frowsy and draggled as the hair of a lodging-house slavey, and her sides were filthy.

"That," said a man of my people, "is a very fair specimen of a Russian. You should see their men-of-war; they are just as filthy. Some of 'em come into Nagasaki to clean."

It was a small piece of information and perhaps untrue, but it put the roof to my good humour as I stepped on to the bund and was told in faultless English by a young gentleman, with a plated chrysanthemum in his forage cap and badly fitting German uniform on his limbs, that he did not understand my language. He was a Japanese customs official. Had our stay been longer, I would have wept over him because he was a hybrid—partly French, partly German, and partly American—a tribute to civilisation. All the Japanese officials from police upwards seem to be clad in Europe clothes, and never do those clothes fit. I think the Mikado made them at the same time as the Constitution. They will come right in time.

When the 'rickshaw, drawn by a beautiful apple-cheeked young man with a Basque face, shot me into the *Mikado*, First Act, I did not stop and shout with delight, because the dignity of India was in my keeping. I lay back on the velvet cushions and grinned luxuriously at Pittising, with her sash and three giant hair-pins in her blue-black hair, and three-inch clogs on her feet. She laughed—even as did the Burmese girl in the old Pagoda at Moulmein. And her laugh, the laugh of a lady, was my welcome to Japan. Can the people help laughing? I think not. You see they have such thousands of children in their streets that the elders must perforce be young lest the babes should grieve. Nagasaki is inhabited entirely by children. The grown-ups exist on sufferance.

A four-foot child walks with a three-foot child, who is holding the hand of a two-foot child, who carries on her back a one-foot child, who — but you will not believe me if I say that the scale runs down to six-inch little Jap dolls such as they used to sell in the Burlington Arcade. These dolls wriggle and laugh. They are tied up in a blue bed-gown which is tied by a sash, which again ties up the bed-gown of the carrier. Thus if you untie that sash, baby and but little bigger brother are at once perfectly naked. I saw a mother do this, and it was for all the world like the peeling of hard-boiled eggs.

If you look for extravagance of colour, for flaming shop fronts and glaring lanterns, you shall find none of these things in the narrow stone-paved streets of Naga-saki. But if you desire details of house construction, glimpses of perfect cleanliness, rare taste, and perfect sub ordination of the thing made to the needs of the maker, you shall find all you seek and more. All the roofs are dull lead colour, being shingled or tiled, and all the house fronts are of the colour of the wood as God made it. There is neither smoke nor haze, and in the clear light of a clouded sky I could see down the narrowest alley-way as into the interior of a cabinet.

The books have long ago told you how a Japanese house is constructed, chiefly of sliding screens and paper partitions, and everybody knows the story of the burglar of Tokio who burgled with a pair of scissors for jimmy and centrebit and stole the Consul's trousers. But all the telling in print will never make you understand the exquisite finish of a tenement that you could kick in with your foot and pound to match-wood with your fists. Be-hold a *bunnia's* [1] shop. He sells rice and chillies and dried

[1] grain-dealer's.

fish and wooden scoops made of bamboo. The front of
his shop is very solid. It is made of half-inch battens
nailed side by side. Not one of the battens is broken;
and each one is foursquare perfectly. Feeling ashamed
of himself for this surly barring up of his house, he fills
one-half the frontage with oiled paper stretched upon
quarter-inch framing. Not a single square of oil paper
has a hole in it, and not one of the squares, which in more
uncivilised countries would hold a pane of glass if strong
enough, is out of line. And the *bunnia*, clothed in a blue
dressing-gown, with thick white stockings on his feet, sits
behind, not among his wares, on a pale gold-coloured mat
of soft rice straw bound with black list at the edges.
This mat is two inches thick, three feet wide and six
long. You might, if you were a sufficient pig, eat your
dinner off any portion of it. The *bunnia* lies with
one wadded blue arm round a big brazier of hammered
brass on which is faintly delineated in incised lines
a very terrible dragon. The brazier is full of charcoal
ash, but there is no ash on the mat. By the *bunnia's*
side is a pouch of green leather tied with a red silk
cord, holding tobacco cut fine as cotton. He fills a
long black and red lacquered pipe, lights it at the
charcoal in the brazier, takes two whiffs, and the pipe is
empty. Still there is no speck on the mat. Behind the
bunnia is a shadow-screen of bead and bamboo. This
veils a room floored with pale gold and roofed with panels
of grained cedar. There is nothing in the room save a
blood-red blanket laid out smoothly as a sheet of paper.
Beyond the room is a passage of polished wood, so polished that it gives back the reflections of the white paper
wall. At the end of the passage and clearly visible to

this unique *bunnia* is a dwarfed pine two feet high in a green glazed pot, and by its side is a branch of azalea, blood red as the blanket, set in a pale grey crackle-pot. The *bunnia* has put it there for his own pleasure, for the delight of his eyes, because he loves it. The white man has nothing whatever to do with his tastes, and he keeps his house specklessly pure because he likes cleanliness and knows it is artistic. What shall we say to such a *bunnia?*

His brother in Northern India may live behind a front of time-blackened open-work wood, but . . . I do not think he would grow anything save *tulsi*[1] in a pot, and that only to please the Gods and his womenfolk.

Let us not compare the two men, but go on through Nagasaki.

Except for the horrible policemen who insist on being Continental, the people — the common people, that is — do not run after unseemly costumes of the West. The young men wear round felt hats, occasionally coats and trousers, and semi-occasionally boots. All these are vile. In the more metropolitan towns men say Western dress is rather the rule than the exception. If this be so, I am disposed to conclude that the sins of their forefathers in making enterprising Jesuit missionaries into beefsteak have been visited on the Japanese in the shape of a partial obscuration of their artistic instincts. Yet the punishment seems rather too heavy for the offence.

Then I fell admiring the bloom on the people's cheeks, the three-cornered smiles of the fat babes, and the surpassing "otherness" of everything round me. It is so strange to be in a clean land, and stranger to walk among doll's houses. Japan is a soothing place for a

[1] A sacred herb of the Hindus.

small man. Nobody comes to tower over him, and he looks down upon all the women, as is right and proper. A dealer in curiosities bent himself double on his own door-mat, and I passed in, feeling for the first time that I was a barbarian, and no true Sahib. The slush of the streets was thick on my boots, and he, the immaculate owner, asked me to walk across a polished floor and white mats to an inner chamber. He brought me a foot-mat, which only made matters worse, for a pretty girl giggled round the corner as I toiled at it. Japanese shopkeepers ought not to be so clean. I went into a boarded passage about two feet wide, found a gem of a garden of dwarfed trees, in the space of half a tennis court, whacked my head on a fragile lintel, and arrived at a four-walled daintiness where I involuntarily lowered my voice. Do you recollect Mrs. Molesworth's *Cuckoo Clock*, and the big cabinet that Griselda entered with the cuckoo? I was not Griselda, but my low-voiced friend, in his long, soft wraps, was the cuckoo, and the room was the cabinet. Again I tried to console myself with the thought that I could kick the place to pieces; but this only made me feel large and coarse and dirty, — a most unfavourable mood for bargaining. The cuckoo-man caused pale tea to be brought, — just such tea as you read of in books of travel, — and the tea completed my embarrassment. What I wanted to say was, "Look here, you person. You're much too clean and refined for this life here below, and your house is unfit for a man to live in until he has been taught a lot of things which I have never learned. Consequently I hate you because I feel myself your inferior, and you despise me and my boot, because you know me for a savage. Let me go, or I'll pull your house of cedar-wood over your ears." What I really said was, "Oh, ah yes. Awf'ly pretty. Awful queer way of doing business."

The cuckoo-man proved to be a horrid extortioner; but I was hot and uncomfortable till I got outside, and was a bog-trotting Briton once more. You have never blundered into the inside of a three-hundred-dollar cabinet, therefore you will not understand me.

We came to the foot of a hill, as it might have been the hill on which the Shway Dagon stands, and up that hill ran a mighty flight of grey, weather-darkened steps, spanned here and there by monolithic *torii*. Every one knows what a *torii* is. They have them in Southern India. A great King makes a note of the place where he intends to build a huge arch, but being a King does so in stone, not ink — sketches in the air two beams and a cross-bar, forty or sixty feet high, and twenty or thirty wide. In Southern India the cross-bar is humped in the middle. In the Further East it flares up at the ends. This description is hardly according to the books, but if a man begins by consulting books in a new country he is lost. Over the steps hung heavy blue-green or green-black pines, old, gnarled, and bossed. The foliage of the hillside was a lighter green, but the pines set the keynote of colour, and the blue dresses of the few folk on the steps answered it. There was no sunshine in the air, but I vow that sunshine would have spoilt all. We climb for five minutes, — I and the Professor and the camera, — and then we turned, and saw the roofs of Nagasaki lying at our feet — a sea of lead and dull-brown, with here and there a smudge of creamy pink to mark the bloom of the cherry trees. The hills round the town were speckled with the resting-places of the dead, with clumps of pine and feathery bamboo.

"What a country!" said the Professor, unstrapping his camera. "And have you noticed, wherever we go there's always some man who knows how to carry my kit? The *gharri* driver at Moulmein handed me my stops; the fellow at Penang knew all about it, too; and the 'rickshaw coolie has seen a camera before. Curious, isn't it?"

"Professor," said I, "it's due to the extraordinary fact that we are not the only people in the world. I began to realise it at Hong-Kong. It's getting plainer now. I shouldn't be surprised if we turned out to be ordinary human beings, after all."

We entered a courtyard where an evil-looking bronze horse stared at two stone lions, and a company of children babbled among themselves. There is a legend connected with the bronze horse, which may be found in the guide-books. But the real true story of the creature is, that he was made long ago out of the fossil ivory of Siberia by a Japanese Prometheus, and got life and many foals, whose descendants closely resemble their father. Long years have almost eliminated the ivory in the blood, but it crops out in creamy mane and tail; and the pot-belly and marvellous feet of the bronze horse may be found to this day among the pack ponies of Nagasaki, who carry pack-saddles adorned with velvet and red cloth, who wear grass shoes on their hind feet, and who are made like to horses in a pantomime.

We could not go beyond this courtyard because a label said, "No admittance," and thus all we saw of the temple was rich-brown high roofs of blackened thatch, breaking back and back in wave and undulation till they were lost in the foliage. The Japanese can play with thatch as men play with modelling clay, but how their light underpinnings can carry the weight of the roof is a mystery to the lay eye.

We went down the steps to tiffin, and a half-formed resolve was shaping itself in my heart the while. Burma was a very nice place, but they eat *gnapi* there, and there were smells, and after all, the girls weren't so pretty as some others —

" You must take off your boots," said Y-Tokai.

I assure you there is no dignity in sitting down on the steps of a tea-house and struggling with muddy boots. And it is impossible to be polite in your stockinged feet when the floor under you is as smooth as glass and a pretty girl wants to know where you would like tiffin. Take at least one pair of beautiful socks with you when you come this way. Get them made of embroidered *sambhur* skin, of silk if you like, but do not stand as I did in cheap striped brown things with a darn at the heel, and try to talk to a tea-girl.

They led us — three of them, and all fresh and pretty — into a room furnished with a golden-brown bearskin. The *tokonoma*, recess aforementioned, held one scroll-picture of bats wheeling in the twilight, a bamboo flower-holder, and yellow flowers. The ceiling was of panelled wood, with the exception of one strip at the side nearest the window, and this was made of plaited shavings of cedar-wood, marked off from the rest of the ceiling by a wine-brown bamboo so polished that it might have been lacquered. A touch of the hand sent one side of the room flying back, and we entered a really large room

with another *tokonoma* framed on one side by eight or ten
feet of an unknown wood, bearing the same grain as a
Penang lawyer, and above by a stick of unbarked tree set
there purely because it was curiously mottled.   In this
second *tokonoma* was a pearl-grey vase, and that was all.
Two sides of the room were of oiled paper, and the joints
of the beams were covered by the brazen images of crabs,
half life-size.   Save for the sill of the *tokonoma,* which
was black lacquer, every inch of wood in the place was
natural grain without flaw.   Outside was the garden,
fringed with a hedge of dwarf-pines and adorned with a
tiny pond, water-smoothed stones sunk in the soil, and
a blossoming cherry tree.

They left us alone in this paradise of cleanliness and
beauty, and being only a shameless Englishman without
his boots — a white man is always degraded when he goes
barefoot — I wandered round the wall, trying all the
screens. It was only when I stooped to examine the sunk
catch of a screen that I saw it was a plaque of inlay
work representing two white cranes feeding on fish. The
whole was about three inches square and in the ordinary
course of events would never be looked at.   The screens
hid a cupboard in which all the lamps and candlesticks
and pillows and sleeping-bags of the household seemed
to be stored. An Oriental nation that can fill a cupboard
tidily is a nation to bow down to.   Upstairs I went by a
staircase of grained wood and lacquer, into rooms of
rarest device with circular windows that opened on
nothing, and so were filled with bamboo tracery for the
delight of the eye.   The passages floored with dark wood
shone like ice, and I was ashamed.

"Professor," said I, "they don't spit; they don't eat

like pigs; they can't quarrel, and a drunken man would reel straight through every portion in the house and roll down the hill into Nagasaki. They can't have any children." Here I stopped. Downstairs was full of babies.

The maidens came in with tea in blue china and cake in a red lacquered bowl — such cake as one gets at one or two houses in Simla. We sprawled ungracefully on red rugs over the mats, and they gave us chopsticks to separate the cake with. It was a long task.

"Is that all?" growled the Professor. "I'm hungry, and cake and tea oughtn't to come till four o'clock." Here he took a wedge of cake furtively with his hands.

They returned — five of them this time — with black lacquer stands a foot square and four inches high. Those were our tables. They bore a red lacquered bowlful of fish boiled in brine, and sea-anemones. At least they were not mushrooms. A paper napkin tied with gold thread enclosed our chopsticks; and in a little flat saucer lay a smoked crayfish, a slice of a compromise that looked like Yorkshire pudding and tasted like sweet omelette, and a twisted fragment of some translucent thing that had once been alive but was now pickled. They went away, but not empty handed, for thou, oh, O-Toyo, didst take away my heart — same which I gave to the Burmese girl in the Shway Dagon pagoda!

The Professor opened his eyes a little, but said no word. The chopsticks demanded all his attention, and the return of the girls took up the rest. O-Toyo, ebon-haired, rosy-cheeked, and made throughout of delicate porcelain, laughed at me because I devoured all the mustard sauce that had been served with my raw fish, and wept copiously till she gave me *saki* from a lordly bottle about four inches high. If you took some very thin hock, and tried to mull it and forgot all about the brew till it was half cold, you would get *saki*. I had mine in a saucer so tiny that I was bold to have it filled eight or ten times and loved O-Toyo none the less at the end.

After raw fish and mustard sauce came some other sort of fish cooked with pickled radishes, and very slippery on the chopsticks. The girls knelt in a semicircle and shrieked with delight at the Professor's clumsiness, for indeed it was not I that nearly upset the dinner table in a vain attempt to recline gracefully. After the bamboo-shoots came a basin of white beans in sweet sauce — very tasty indeed. Try to convey beans to your mouth with a pair of wooden knitting-needles and see what happens. Some chicken cunningly boiled with turnips, and a bowl-ful of snow-white boneless fish and a pile of rice, con-cluded the meal. I have forgotten one or two of the courses, but when O-Toyo handed me the tiny lacquered Japanese pipe full of hay-like tobacco, I counted nine dishes in the lacquer stand — each dish representing a course. Then O-Toyo and I smoked by alternate pipefuls.

My very respectable friends at all the clubs and messes, have you ever after a good tiffin lolled on cushions and smoked, with one pretty girl to fill your pipe and four to admire you in an unknown tongue? You do not know what life is. I looked round me at that faultless room, at the dwarf pines and creamy cherry blossoms without, at O-Toyo bubbling with laughter because I blew smoke through my nose, and at the ring of *Mikado* maidens over against the golden-brown bearskin rug. Here was colour, form, food, comfort, and beauty enough for half a year's contemplation. I would not be a Burman any more. I would be a Japanese — always with O-Toyo — in a cabinet workhouse on a camphor-scented hillside.

"Heigho!" said the Professor. "There are worse places than this to live and die in. D'you know our steamer goes at four? Let's ask for the bill and get away."

Now I have left my heart with O-Toyo under the pines. Perhaps I shall get it back at Kobé.

A FURTHER CONSIDERATION OF JAPAN. THE INLAND SEA,
AND GOOD COOKERY. THE MYSTERY OF PASSPORTS AND
CONSULATES, AND CERTAIN OTHER MATTERS.

"Rome! Rome! Wasn't that the place where I got the good
cigars?"   — *Memoirs of a Traveller.*

ALAS for the incompleteness of the written word!
There was so much more that I meant to tell you about
Nagasaki and the funeral procession that I found in her
streets. You ought to have read about the wailing
women in white who followed the dead man shut up in
a wooden sedan chair that rocked on the shoulders of the
bearers, while the bronze-hued Buddhist priest tramped
on ahead, and the little boys ran alongside.

I had prepared in my mind moral reflections, purviews
of political situations, and a complete essay on the future
of Japan. Now I have forgotten everything except
O-Toyo in the tea-garden.

From Nagasaki we — the P. and O. Steamer — are going to Kobé by way of the Inland Sea. That is to say,
we have for the last twenty hours been steaming through
a huge lake, studded as far as the eye can reach with
islands of every size, from four miles long and two wide
to little cocked-hat hummocks no bigger than a decent
hayrick. Messrs. Cook and Son charge about one hundred rupees extra for the run through this part of the

world, but they do not know how to farm the beauties of nature. Under any skies the islands — purple, amber, grey, green, and black — are worth five times the money asked. I have been sitting for the last half-hour among a knot of whooping tourists, wondering how I could give you a notion of them. The tourists, of course, are indescribable. They say, "Oh my!" at thirty-second intervals, and at the end of five minutes call one to another: "Sa-ay, don't you think it's vurry much the same all along?" Then they play cricket with a broomstick till an unusually fair prospect makes them stop and shout "Oh my!" again. If there were a few more oaks and pines on the islands, the run would be three hundred miles of Naini Tal lake. But we are not near Naini Tal; for as the big ship drives down the alleys of water, I can see the heads of the breakers flying ten feet up the side of the echoing cliffs, albeit the sea is dead-still.

Now we have come to a stretch so densely populated with islands that all looks solid ground. We are running through broken water thrown up by the race of the tide round an outlying reef, and apparently are going to hit an acre of solid rock. Somebody on the bridge saves us, and we head out for another island, and so on, and so on, till the eye wearies of watching the nose of the ship swinging right and left, and the finite human soul, which, after all, cannot repeat "Oh my!" through a chilly evening, goes below. When you come to Japan — it can be done comfortably in three months, or even ten weeks — sail through this marvellous sea, and see how quickly wonder sinks to interest, and interest to apathy. We brought oysters with us from Nagasaki. I am much more interested in their appearance at dinner to night than in the shag-backed starfish of an islet that has just slidden by like a ghost upon the silver-grey waters, awakening under the touch of the ripe moon. Yes, it is a sea of mystery and romance, and the white sails of the junks are silver in the moonlight. But if the steward curries those oysters instead of serving them on the shell, all the veiled beauties of cliff and water-carven rock will not console me. To-day being the seventeenth of April, I am sitting in an ulster under a thick rug, with fingers so cold I can barely hold the pen. This emboldens me to ask how your thermantidotes are working. A mixture of steatite and kerosene is very good for creaking cranks, I believe, and if the coolie falls asleep, and you wake up in Hades, try not to lose your temper. I go to my oysters.

Two days later. This comes from Kobé (thirty hours from Nagasaki), the European portion of which is a raw American town. We walked down the wide, naked streets between houses of sham stucco, with Corinthian pillars of wood, wooden verandahs and piazzas, all stony grey beneath stony grey skies, and keeping guard over raw green saplings miscalled shade trees. In truth, Kobé is hideously American in externals. Even I, who have only seen pictures of America, recognised at once that it was Portland, Maine. It lives among hills, but the hills are all scalped, and the general impression is of out-of-the-wayness. Yet, ere I go further, let me sing the praises of the excellent M. Begeux, proprietor of the Oriental Hotel, upon whom be peace. His is a house where you can dine. He does not merely feed you. His coffee is the coffee of the beautiful France. For tea he gives you Peliti cakes (but better) and the *vin ordinaire* which is *compris*, is good. Excellent Monsieur and Madame Begeux! If the *Pioneer* were a medium for puffs, I would write a leading article upon your potato salad, your beefsteaks, your fried fish, and your staff of highly trained Japanese servants in blue tights, who looked like so many small Hamlets without the velvet cloak, and who obeyed the unspoken wish. No, it should be a poem — a ballad of good living. I have eaten curries of the rarest at the Oriental at Penang, the turtle steaks of Raffles's at Singapur still live in my regretful memory, and they gave me chicken liver and sucking-pig in the Victoria at Hong-Kong which I will always extol. But the Oriental at Kobé was better than all three. Remember this, and so shall you who come after slide round a quarter of the world upon a sleek and contented stomach.

We are going from Kobé to Yokohama by various roads. This necessitates a passport, because we travel in the interior and do not run round the coast on shipboard. We take a railroad, which may or may not be complete as to the middle, and we branch off from that railroad, complete or not, as the notion may prompt. This will be an affair of some twenty days, and ought to include forty or fifty miles by 'rickshaw, a voyage on a lake, and, I believe, bedbugs. *Nota bene.*—When you come to Japan stop at Hong-Kong and send on a letter to the "Envoy Extraordinary and Minister Plenipotentiary at Tokio," if you want to travel in the interior of this Fairyland. Indicate your route as roughly as ever you choose, but for your own comfort give the two extreme towns you intend to touch. Throw in any details about your age, profession, colour of hair, and the like that may occur to you, and ask to have a passport sent to the British Consulate at Kobé to meet you. Allow the man with a long title a week's time to prepare the passport, and you will find it at your service when you land. Only write distinctly, to save your vanity. My papers are addressed to a Mister Kyshrig — Radjerd Kyshrig.

As in Nagasaki, the town was full of babies, and as in Nagasaki, every one smiled except the Chinamen. I do not like Chinamen. There was something in their faces which I could not understand, though it was familiar enough.

"The Chinaman's a native," I said. "That's the look on a native's face, but the Jap isn't a native, and he isn't a sahib either. What is it?" The Professor considered the surging street for a while.

"The Chinaman's an old man when he's young, just as a native is, but the Jap is a child all his life. Think how grown-up people look among children. That's the look that's puzzling you."

I dare not say that the Professor is right, but to my eyes it seemed he spoke sooth. As the knowledge of good and evil sets its mark upon the face of a grown man of Our people, so something I did not understand had marked the faces of the Chinamen. They had no kinship with the crowd beyond that which a man has to children.

"They are the superior race," said the Professor, ethnologically.

"They can't be. They don't know how to enjoy life," I answered immorally. "And, anyway, their art isn't human."

"What does it matter?" said the Professor. "Here's

a shop full of the wrecks of old Japan.   Let's go in and
look." We went in, but I want somebody to solve the
Chinese question for me. It's too large to handle alone.

We entered the curio-shop aforementioned, with our
hats in our hands, through a small avenue of carved
stone lanterns and wooden sculptures of devils unspeak-
ably hideous, to be received by a smiling image who had
grown grey among *netsukes* and lacquer. He showed us
the banners and insignia of daimios long since dead,
while our jaws drooped in ignorant wonder. He showed
us a sacred turtle of mammoth size, carven in wood down
to minutest detail. Through room after room he led
us, the light fading as we went, till we reached a tiny
garden and a woodwork cloister that ran round it.
Suits of old-time armour made faces at us in the gloom,
ancient swords clicked at our feet, quaint tobacco
pouches as old as the swords swayed to and fro from
some invisible support, and the eyes of a score of battered Buddhas, red dragons, Jain *tirthankars,* and Burmese *beloos* glared at us from over the fence of tattered
gold brocade robes of state. The joy of possession lives
in the eye. The old man showed us his treasures, from
crystal spheres mounted in sea-worn wood to cabinet on
cabinet full of ivory and wood carvings, and we were
as rich as though we owned all that lay before us.
Unfortunately the merest scratch of Japanese characters
is the only clew to the artist's name, so I am unable to
say who conceived, and in creamy ivory executed, the
old man horribly embarrassed by a cuttle-fish; the
priest who made the soldier pick up a deer for him and
laughed to think that the brisket would be his and the
burden his companion's ; or the dry, lean snake coiled

in derision on a jawless skull mottled with the memories
of corruption; or the Rabelaisan badger who stood on
his head and made you blush though he was not half an
inch long ; or the little fat boy pounding his smaller
brother ; or the rabbit that had just made a joke; or —
but there were scores of these notes, born of every mood
of mirth, scorn, and experience that sways the heart of
man; and by this hand that has held half a dozen of
them in its palm I winked at the shade of the dead
carver ! He had gone to his rest, but he had worked out
in ivory three or four impressions that I had been hunting after in cold print.

The Englishman is a wonderful animal. He buys a
dozen of these things and puts them on the top of an
overcrowded cabinet, where they look like blobs of ivory,
and forgets them in a week. The Japanese hides them
in a beautiful brocaded bag or a quiet lacquer box till
three congenial friends come to tea. Then he takes
them out slowly, and they are looked over with appreciation amid quiet chuckles to the deliberative clink of
cups, and put back again till the mood for inspection
returns. That is the way to enjoy what we call curios.
Every man with money is a collector in Japan, but you
shall find no crowds of "things" outside the best shops.

We stayed long in the half-light of that quaint place,
and when we went away we grieved afresh that such
a people should have a "constitution" or should dress
every tenth young man in European clothes, put a white
ironclad in Kobé harbour, and send a dozen myoptic
lieutenants in baggy uniforms about the streets.

"It would pay us," said the Professor, his head in
a clog-shop, "it would pay us to establish an inter-

national suzerainty over Japan to take, away any fear
of invasion or annexation, and pay the country as much
as ever it chose, on condition that it simply sat still and
went on making beautiful things while our men learned.
It would pay us to put the whole Empire in a glass case
and mark it, '*Hors concours,*' Exhibit A."

"H'mm," said I. "Who's us ?"

"Oh, we generally — the *Sahib log* all the world over.
Our workmen — a few of them — can do as good work
in certain lines, but you don't find whole towns full of
clean, capable, dainty, designful people in Europe."

"Let's go to Tokio and speak to the Emperor about
it," I said.

"Let's go to a Japanese theatre first," said the Professor. "It's too early in the tour to start serious
politics."

No. XIII

To the theatre we went, through the mud and much rain. Internally it was nearly dark, for the deep blue of the audience's dress soaked up the scanty light of the kerosene lamps. There was no standing room anywhere except next to the Japanese policeman, who in the cause of morals and the Lord Chamberlain had a corner in the gallery and four chairs all to himself. He was quite four feet eight inches high, and Napoleon at St. Helena could not have folded his arms more dramatically. After some grunting — I fear we were upsetting the principles of the Constitution — he consented to give us one chair, receiving in return a Burma cheroot which I have every reason to believe blew his little head off. A pit containing fifty rows of fifty people and a bonding layer of babies, with a gallery which might have held twelve hundred, made up the house. The building was as delicate a piece of cabinet work as any of the houses; roof, floor, beams, props, verandahs, and partitions were of naked wood, and every other person in the house was smoking a tiny pipe and knocking out the ashes every two minutes. Then I wished to fly; death by the *auto da fe* not being anywhere paid for in the tour; but there

was no escape by the one little door where pickled fish
was being sold between the acts.

"Yes, it's not exactly safe," said the Professor, as the
matches winked and sputtered all round and below
"But if that curtain catches that naked light on the
stage, or you see this matchwood gallery begin to blaze,
I'll kick out the back of the refreshment buffet, and we
can walk away."

With this warm comfort the drama began. The green
curtain dropped from above and was whisked away, and
three gentlemen and a lady opened the ball by a dialogue
conducted in tones between a "burble" and a falsetto
whisper. If you wish to know their costumes, look at
the nearest Japanese fan. Real Japs of course are like
men and women, but stage Japs in their stiff brocades
are line for line as Japs are drawn. When the four sat
down, a little boy ran among them and settled their
draperies, pulling out a sash bow here, displaying a skirt-
fold there. The costumes were as gorgeous as the plot
was incomprehensible. But we will call the play "*The
Thunder Cat, or Harlequin Bag o' Bones and the Amazing
Old Woman, or The Mammoth Radish, or The Superfluous
Badger and the Swinging Lights.*"

A two-sworded man in the black and gcld brocade
rose up and imitated the gait of an obscure actor called
Henry Irving, whereat, not knowing that he was serious,
I cackled aloud till the Japanese policeman looked at
me austerely. Then the two-sworded man wooed the
Japanese-fan lady, the other characters commenting on
his proceedings like a Greek chorus till something —
perhaps a misplaced accent — provoked trouble, and the
two-sworded man and a vermilion splendour enjoyed a

Vincent Crummles fight to the music of all the orchestra
— one guitar and something that clicked — not castanets.
The small boy removed their weapons when the men
had sufficiently warred, and, conceiving that the piece
wanted light, fetched a ten-foot bamboo with a naked
candle at the end, and held this implement about a foot
from the face of the two-sworded man, following his
every movement with the anxious eye of a child in-
trusted with a typewriter. Then the Japanese-fan girl
consented to the wooing of the two-sworded man, and
with a scream of eldritch laughter turned into a hideous
old woman — a boy took off her hair, but she did
the rest herself. At this terrible moment a gilded Thunder Cat, which is a cat issuing from a cloud, ran on wires
from the flies to the centre of the gallery, and a boy with
a badger's tail mocked at the two-sworded man. Then
I knew that the two-sworded man had offended a cat
and a badger, and would have a very bad time of it, for
these two animals and the fox are to this day black sor-
cerers. Fearful things followed, and the scenery was
changed once every five minutes. The prettiest effect
was secured by a double row of candles hung on strings
behind a green gauze far up the stage and set swinging
with opposite motions. This, besides giving a fine idea of
uncanniness, made one member of the audience sea-sick.

But the two-sworded man was far more miserable than
I. The bad Thunder Cat cast such spells upon him that
I gave up trying to find out what he meant to be. He was
a fat-faced low comedian King of the Rats, assisted by
other rats, and he ate a magic radish with side-splitttng
pantomime till he became a man once more. Then all
his bones were taken away, — still by the Thunder Cat, —

and he fell into a horrid heap, illuminated by the small boy with the candle — and would not recover himself till somebody spoke to a magic parrot, and a huge hairy villain and several coolies had walked over him. Then he was a girl, but, hiding behind a parasol, resumed his shape, and then the curtain came down and the audience ran about the stage and circulated generally One small boy took it into his head that he could turn head-over-heels from the Prompt side across. With great gravity, before the unregarding house, he set to work, but rolled over sideways with a flourish of chubby legs. Nobody cared, and the polite people in the gallery could not understand why the Professor and I were helpless with laughter when the child, with a clog for a sword, imitated the strut of the two-sworded man. The actors changed in public, and any one who liked might help shift scenes. Why should not a baby enjoy himself if he liked?

A little later we left. The Thunder Cat was still working her wicked will on the two-sworded man, but all would be set right next day. There was a good deal to be done, but Justice was at the end of it. The man who sold pickled fish and tickets said so.

"Good school for a young actor," said the Professor. "He'd see what unpruned eccentricities naturally develop into. There's every trick and mannerism of the English stage in that place, magnified thirty diameters, but perfectly recognisable. How do you intend to describe it?"

"The Japanese comic opera of the future has yet to be written," I responded, grandiloquently. "Yet to be written in spite of the *Mikado*. The badger has not yet

appeared on an English stage, and the artistic mask as
an accessory to the legitimate drama has never been
utilised. Just imagine the *Thunder Cat* as a title for a
serio-comic opera. Begin with a domestic cat possessed
of magic powers, living in the house of a London tea-
merchant who kicks her. Consider — "

"The lateness of the hour," was the icy answer. "To-
morrow we will go and write operas in the temple close
to this place."

* * * * * * *

To-morrow brought fine drizzling rain. The sun, by
the way, has been hidden now for more than three
weeks. They took us to what must be the chief temple
of Kobé and gave it a name which I do not remember.
It is an exasperating thing to stand at the altars of a
faith that you know nothing about. There be rites and
ceremonies of the Hindu creed that all have read of and
must have witnessed, but in what manner do they pray
here who look to Buddha, and what worship is paid at
the Shinto shrines? The books say one thing; the eyes,
another.

The temple would seem to be also a monastery and a
place of great peace disturbed only by the babble of
scores of little children. It stood back from the road
behind a sturdy wall, an irregular mass of steep pitched
roofs bound fantastically at the crown, copper-green
where the thatch had ripened under the touch of time,
and dull grey-black where the tiles ran. Under the
eaves a man who believed in his God, and so could
do good work, had carved his heart into wood till it blossomed and broke into waves or curled with the ripple of

live flames. Somewhere on the outskirts of Lahore city stands a mazy gathering of tombs and cloister walks called Chajju Bhagat's Chubara, built no one knows when and decaying no one cares how soon. Though this temple was large and spotlessly clean within and without, the silence and rest of the place were those of the courtyards in the far-off Punjab. The priests had made many gardens in corners of the wall — gardens perhaps forty feet long by twenty wide, and each, though different from its neighbour, containing a little pond with goldfish, a stone lantern or two, hummocks of rock, flat stones carved with inscriptions, and a cherry or peach tree all blossom.

Stone-paved paths ran across the courtyard and connected building with building. In an inner enclosure, where lay the prettiest garden of all, was a golden tablet ten or twelve feet high, against which stood in high relief of hammered bronze the figure of a goddess in flowing robes. The space between the paved paths here was strewn with snowy-white pebbles, and in white pebbles on red they had written on the ground, "How happy." You might take them as you pleased — for the sigh of contentment or the question of despair.

The temple itself, reached by a wooden bridge, was nearly dark, but there was light enough to show a hundred subdued splendours of brown and gold, of silk and faithfully painted screen. If you have once seen a Buddhist altar where the Master of the Law sits among golden bells, ancient bronzes, flowers in vases, and banners of tapestry, you will begin to understand why the Roman Catholic Church once prospered so mightily in this country, and will prosper in all lands where it finds an elaborate ritual already existing. An art-loving folk will have a God who is to be propitiated with pretty things as surely as a race bred among rocks and moors and driving clouds will enshrine their deity in the storm, and make him the austere recipient of the sacrifice of the rebellious human spirit. Do you remember the story of the Bad People of Iquique? The man who told me that yarn told me another — of the Good People of Somewhere Else. They also were simple South Americans with nothing to wear, and had been conducting a service of their own in honour of their God before a black-jowled Jesuit father. At a critical moment some one forgot the ritual, or a monkey invaded the sanctity of that forest shrine and stole the priest's only garment. Anyhow, an absurdity happened, and the Good People burst into shouts of laughter and broke off to play for a while.

"But what will your God say?" asked the Jesuit, scandalised at the levity.

"Oh! he knows everything. He knows that we forget, and can't attend, and do it all wrong, but He is very wise and very strong," was the reply.

"Well, that doesn't excuse you."

"Of course it does. He just lies back and laughs," said the Good People of Somewhere Else, and fell to pelting each other with blossoms.

I forget what is the precise bearing of this anecdote. But to return to the temple. Hidden away behind a mass of variegated gorgeousness was a row of very familiar figures with gold crowns on their heads. One does not expect to meet Krishna the Butter Thief and Kali the husband beater so far east as Japan.

"What are these?"

"They are other gods," said a young priest, who giggled deprecatingly at his own creed every time he was questioned about it. "They are very old. They came from India in the past. I think they are Indian gods, but I do not know why they are here."

I hate a man who is ashamed of his faith. There was a story connected with those gods, and the priest would not tell it to me. So I sniffed at him scornfully, and went my way. It led me from the temple straight into the monastery, which was all made of delicate screens, polished floors, and brown wood ceilings. Except for my tread on the boards there was no sound in the place till I heard some one breathing heavily behind a screen. The priest slid back what had appeared to me a dead wall, and we found a very old priest half-asleep over his charcoal handwarmer. This was the picture. The priest in olive-green, his bald head, pure silver, bowed down before a sliding screen of white oiled paper which let in dull silver light. To his right a battered black lacquer stand containing the Indian ink and brushes with which he feigned to work. To the right of these, again, a pale yellow bamboo table holding a vase of olive-green crackle, and a sprig of almost black pine. There were no blossoms in this place. The priest was too old. Behind the sombre picture stood a gorgeous little Buddhist shrine,—gold and vermilion.

"He makes a fresh picture for the little screen here every day," said the young priest, pointing first to his senior, and then to a blank little tablet on the wall. The old man laughed pitifully, rubbed his head, and handed me his picture for the day. It represented a

flood over rocky ground; two men in a boat were helping two others on a tree half-submerged by the water.
Even I could tell that the power had gone from him.
He must have drawn well in his manhood, for one figure
in the boat had action and purpose as it leaned over the
gunwale; but the rest was blurred, and the lines had
wandered astray as the poor old hand had quavered
across the paper. I had no time to wish the artist a
pleasant old age, and an easy death in the great peace
that surrounded him, before the young man drew me
away to the back of the shrine, and showed me a second
smaller altar facing shelves on shelves of little gold and
lacquer tablets covered with Japanese characters.

"These are memorial tablets of the dead," he giggled.
"Once and again the priest he prays here—for those
who are dead, you understand?"

"Perfectly. They call 'em masses where I come
from. I want to go away and think about things. You
shouldn't laugh, though, when you show off your creed."

"Ha, ha!" said the young priest, and I ran away
down the dark polished passages with the faded screens
on either hand, and got into the main courtyard facing
the street, while the Professor was trying to catch temple
fronts with his camera.

A procession passed, four abreast tramping through the
sloshy mud. They did not laugh, which was strange, till
I saw and heard a company of women in white walking
in front of a little wooden palanquin carried on the
shoulders of four bearers and suspiciously light. They
sang a song, half under their breaths—a wailing, moan-
ing song that I had only heard once before, from the
lips of a native far away in the north of India, who had

been clawed past hope of cure by a bear, and was singing his own death-song as his friends bore him along.

"Have makee die," said my 'rickshaw coolie. "Few yu-ne-ral."

I was aware of the fact. Men, women, and little children poured along the streets, and when the death-song died down, helped it forward. The half-mourners wore only pieces of white cloth about their shoulders. The immediate relatives of the dead were in white from head to foot. "Aho! Ahaa! Aho!" they wailed very softly, for fear of breaking the cadence of the falling rain, and they disappeared. All except one old woman, who could not keep pace with the procession, and so came along alone, crooning softly to herself. "Aho! Ahaa! Aho!" she whispered.

The little children in the courtyard were clustered round the Professor's camera. But one child had a very bad skin disease on his innocent head, — so bad that none of the others would play with him, — and he stood in a corner and sobbed and sobbed as though his heart would break. Poor little Gehazi!

EXPLAINS IN WHAT MANNER I WAS TAKEN TO VENICE IN
THE RAIN, AND CLIMBED INTO A DEVIL FORT; A TIN-
POT EXHIBITION, AND A BATH. OF THE MAIDEN AND
THE BOLTLESS DOOR, THE CULTIVATOR AND HIS FIELDS,
AND THE MANUFACTURE OF ETHNOLOGICAL THEORIES
AT RAILROAD SPEED. ENDS WITH KIOTO.

"There's a deal o' fine confused feedin' about sheep's head."
— *Christopher North.*

" COME along to Osaka," said the Professor.

"Why? I'm quite comfy here, and we shall have
lobster cutlets for tiffin; and, anyhow, it is raining
heavily, and we shall get wet."

Sorely against my will — for it was in my mind to
fudge Japan from a guide-book while I enjoyed the
cookery of the Oriental at Kobé — I was dragged into
a 'rickshaw and the rain, and conveyed to a railway
station. Even the Japanese cannot make their railway
stations lovely, though they do their best. Their system
of baggage-booking is borrowed from the Americans;
their narrow-gauge lines, locos, and rolling stock are
English; their passenger-traffic is regulated with the
precision of the Gaul, and the uniforms of their officials
come from the nearest ragbag. The passengers themselves were altogether delightful. A large number of
them were modified Europeans, and resembled nothing

more than Tenniel's picture of the White Rabbit on the first page of *Alice in Wonderland*. They were dressed in neat little tweed suits with fawn-coloured overcoats, and they carried ladies' reticules of black leather and nickel platings. They wore paper and celluloid stuck-up collars which must have been quite thirteen inches round the neck, and their boots were number fours. On their hands — their wee-wee hands — they had white cotton gloves, and they smoked cigarettes from fairy little cigarette cases. That was young Japan — the Japan of the present day.

"Wah, wah, God is great," said the Professor. "But it isn't in human nature for a man who sprawls about on soft mats by instinct to wear Europe clothes as though they belonged to him. If you notice, the last thing that they take to is shoes.

A lapis-lazuli coloured locomotive which, by accident, had a mixed train attached to it happened to loaf up to the platform just then, and we entered a first-class English compartment. There was no stupid double roof, window shade, or abortive thermantidote. It was a London and South-Western carriage. Osaka is about eighteen miles from Kobé, and stands at the head of the bay of Osaka. The train is allowed to go as fast as fifteen miles an hour and to play at the stations all along the line. You must know that the line runs between the hills and the shore, and the drainage-fall is a great deal steeper than anything we have between Saharunpur and Umballa. The rivers and the hill torrents come down straight from the hills on raised beds of their own formation, which beds again have to be bunded and spanned with girder bridges or — here, perhaps, I may be wrong — tunnelled.

The stations are black-tiled, red-walled, and concrete-floored, and all the plant from signal levers to goods-truck is English. The official colour of the bridges is a yellow-brown most like unto a faded chrysanthemum The uniform of the ticket-collectors is a peaked forage cap with gold lines, black frock-coat with brass buttons, very long in the skirt, trousers with black mohair braid, and buttoned kid boots. You cannot be rude to a man in such raiment.

But the countryside was the thing that made us open our eyes. Imagine a land of rich black soil, very heavily manured, and worked by the spade and hoe almost exclusively, and if you split your field (of vision) into half-acre plots, you will get a notion of the raw material the cultivator works on. But all I can write will give you no notion of the wantonness of neatness visible in the fields, of the elaborate system of irrigation, and the mathematical precision of the planting. There was no mixing of crops, no waste of boundary in footpath, and no difference of value in the land. The water stood everywhere within ten feet of the surface, as the well-sweeps attested. On the slopes of the foot-hills each drop between the levels was neatly riveted with unmortared stones, and the edges of the watercuts were faced in like manner. The young rice was transplanted very much as draughts are laid on the board; the tea might have been cropped garden box; and between the lines of the mustard the water lay in the drills as in a wooden trough, while the purple of the beans ran up to the mustard and stopped as though cut with a rule.

On the seaboard we saw an almost continuous line

of towns variegated with factory chimneys ; inland, the crazy-quilt of green, dark-green and gold. Even in the rain the view was lovely, and exactly as Japanese pictures had led me to hope for. Only one drawback occurred to the Professor and myself at the same time. Crops don't grow to the full limit of the seed on heavily worked ground dotted with villages except at a price.

"Cholera ? " said I, watching a stretch of well-sweeps.

"Cholera," said the Professor. " Must be, y'know. It's all sewage irrigation."

I felt that I was friends with the cultivators at once. These broad-hatted, blue-clad gentlemen who tilled their fields by hand — except when they borrowed the village buffalo to drive the share through the rice-slough — knew what the scourge meant.

"How much do you think the Government takes in revenue from vegetable gardens of that kind ? " I demanded.

"Bosh," said he, quietly, " you aren't going to describe the land-tenure of Japan. Look at the yellow of the mustard ! "

It lay in sheets round the line. It ran up the hills to the dark pines. It rioted over the brown sandbars of the swollen rivers, and faded away by mile after mile to the shores of the leaden sea. The high-peaked houses of brown thatch stood knee-deep in it, and it surged up to the factory chimneys of Osaka.

"Great place, Osaka," said the guide. " All sorts of manufactures there."

Osaka is built into and over and among one thousand eight hundred and ninety-four canals, rivers, dams, and watercuts. What the multitudinous chimneys mean I cannot tell. They have something to do with rice and cotton; but it is not good that the Japs should indulge in trade, and I will not call Osaka a "great commercial *entrepot.*" "People who live in paper houses should never sell goods," as the proverb says.

Because of his many wants there is but one hotel for the Englishman in Osaka, and they call it Juter's. Here the views of two civilisations collide and the result is awful. The building is altogether Japanese; wood and tile and sliding screen from top to bottom; but the fitments are mixed. My room, for instance, held a *tokonoma,* made of the polished black stem of a palm and delicate woodwork, framing a scroll picture representing storks. But on the floor over the white mats lay a Brussels carpet that made the indignant toes tingle. From the back verandah one overhung the river which ran straight as an arrow between two lines of houses. They have cabinet-makers in Japan to fit the rivers to the towns. From my verandah I could see three bridges — one a hideous lattice-girder arrangement — and part of a fourth. We were on an island and owned a watergate if we wanted to take a boat.

Apropos of water, be pleased to listen to a Shocking Story. It is written in all the books that the Japanese though cleanly are somewhat casual in their customs. They bathe often with nothing on and together. This notion my experience of the country, gathered in the seclusion of the Oriental at Kobé, made me scoff at. I demanded a tub at Juter's. The infinitesimal man led me down verandahs and upstairs to a beautiful bath-house full of hot and cold water and fitted with cabinet

work, somewhere in a lonely out-gallery. There was
naturally no bolt to the door any more than there would
be a bolt to a dining-room. Had I been sheltered by
the walls of a big Europe bath, I should not have cared,
but I was preparing to wash when a pretty maiden
opened the door, and indicated that she also would tub
in the deep, sunken Japanese bath at my side. When
one is dressed only in one's virtue and a pair of spectacles it is difficult to shut the door in the face of a
girl. She gathered that I was not happy, and withdrew giggling, while I thanked heaven, blushing pro-
fusely the while, that I had been brought up in a
society which unfits a man to bathe *à deux*. Even an
experience of the Paddington Swimming Baths would
have helped me; but coming straight from India Lady
Godiva was a ballet-girl in sentiment compared to this
Actæon.

It rained monsoonishly, and the Professor discovered
a castle which he needs must see. "It's Osaka Castle,"
he said, "and it has been fought over for hundreds of
years. Come along."

"I've seen castles in India. Raighur, Jodhpur — all
sorts of places. Let's have some more boiled salmon.
It's good in this station."

"Pig," said the Professor.

We threaded our way over the four thousand and
fifty-two canals, etc., where the little children played
with the swiftly running water, and never a mother said
"don't," till our 'rickshaw stopped outside a fort ditch
thirty feet deep, and faced with gigantic granite slabs.
On the far side uprose the walls of a fort. But such a
fort! Fifty feet was the height of the wall, and never

a pinch of mortar in the whole. Nor was the face per-
pendicular, but curved like the ram of a man-of-war.
They know the curve in China, and I have seen French
artists introduce it into books describing a devil-besieged
city of Tartary. Possibly everybody else knows it too,
but that is not my affair; life as I have said being altogether new to me. The stone was granite, and the
men of old time had used it like mud. The dressed
blocks that made the profile of the angles were from
twenty feet long, ten or twelve feet high, and as many
in thickness. There was no attempt at binding, but
there was no fault in the jointing.

"And the little Japs built this!" I cried, awe-stricken
at the quarries that rose round me.

"Cyclopean masonry," grunted the Professor, punch-
ing with a stick a monolith of seventeen feet cube.
"Not only did they build it, but they took it. Look
at this. Fire!"

The stones had been split and bronzed in places, and
the cleavage was the cleavage of fire. Evil must it
have been for the armies that led the assault on these
monstrous walls. Castles in India I know, and the forts
of great Emperors I had seen, but neither Akbar in the
north, nor Scindia in the south, had built after this
fashion — without ornament, without colour, but with
a single eye to savage strength and the utmost purity
of line. Perhaps the fort would have looked less for-
bidding in sunlight. The grey, rain-laden atmosphere
through which I saw it suited its spirit. The barracks
of the garrison, the commandant's very dainty house,
a peach-garden, and two deer were foreign to the place.
They should have peopled it with giants from the moun-

tains, instead of — Gurkhas! A Jap infantryman is not
a Gurkha, though he might be mistaken for one as long
as he stood still. The sentry at the quarter-guard belonged, I fancy, to the 4th Regiment. His uniform was
black or blue, with red facings, and shoulder-straps carrying the number of the regiment in cloth. The rain
necessitated an overcoat, but why he should have carried
knapsack, blanket, boots, *and* binoculars I could not
fathom. The knapsack was of cowskin with the hair
on, the boots were strapped soles, cut on each side,
while a heavy country blanket was rolled U-shape over
the head of the knapsack, fitting close to the back. In
the place usually occupied by the mess-tin was a black
leather case shaped like a field-glass. This must be a
mistake of mine, but I can only record as I see. The
rifle was a side-bolt weapon of some kind, and the
bayonet an uncommonly good sword one, locked to the
muzzle, English fashion. The ammunition pouches, as
far as I could see under the greatcoat, ran on the belt in
front, and were double-strapped down. White spatter-
dashes — very dirty — and peaked cap completed the
outfit. I surveyed the man with interest, and would
have made further examination of him but for fear of
the big bayonet. His arms were well kept, — not speck-
less by any means, — but his uniform would have made
an English colonel swear. There was no portion of his
body except the neck that it pretended to fit. I peeped
into the quarter-guard. Fans and dainty tea-sets do not
go with one's notions of a barrack. One drunken defaulter of certain far-away regiments that I could name
would not only have cleared out that quarter-guard, but
brought away all its fittings except the rifle-racks. Yet

the little men, who were always gentle, and never got drunk, were mounting guard over a pile that, with a blue fire on the bastions, might have served for the guard-gates of Hell.

I climbed to the top of the fort and was rewarded by a view of thirty miles of country, chiefly pale yellow mustard and blue-green pine, and the sight of the very large city of Osaka fading away into mist. The guide took most pleasure in the factory chimneys. "There is an exposition here — an exposition of industrialities. Come and see," said he. He took us down from that high place and showed us the glory of the land in the shape of corkscrews, tin mugs, egg-whisks, dippers, silks, buttons, and all the trumpery that can be stitched on a card and sold for five-pence three farthings. The Japanese unfortunately make all these things for themselves, and are proud of it. They have nothing to learn from the West as far as finish is concerned, and by intuition know how to case and mount wares tastefully. The exposition was in four large sheds running round a central building which held only screens, pottery, and cabinet-ware loaned for the occasion. I rejoiced to see that the common people did not care for the penknives, and the pencils, and the mock jewellery. They left those sheds alone and discussed the screens, first taking off their clogs that the inlaid floor of the room might not suffer. Of all the gracious things I beheld, two only remain in my memory, — one a screen in grey representing the heads of six devils instinct with malice and hate; the other, a bold sketch in monochrome of an old woodcutter wrestling with the down-bent branch of a tree. Two hundred years have passed since the artist dropped his pencil, but you may almost hear the tough wood jar under the stroke of the chopper, as the old man puts his back into the task and draws in the labouring breath. There is a picture by Legros of a beggar dying in a ditch, which might have been suggested by that screen.

Next morning, after a night's rain, which sent the river racing under the frail balconies at eight miles an hour, the sun broke through the clouds. Is this a little matter to you who can count upon him daily? I had not seen him since March, and was beginning to feel anxious. Then the land of peach blossom spread its draggled wings abroad and rejoiced. All the pretty maidens put on their loveliest crêpe sashes, — fawn colour, pink, blue, orange, and lilac, — all the little children picked up a baby each, and went out to be happy. In a temple garden full of blossom I performed the miracle of Deucalion with two cents' worth of sweets. The babies swarmed on the instant, till, for fear of raising all the mothers too, I forbore to give them any more. They smiled and nodded prettily, and trotted after me, forty strong, the big ones helping the little, and the little ones skipping in the puddles. A Jap child never cries, never scuffles, never fights, and never makes mud pies except when it lives on the banks of a canal. Yet, lest it should spread its sash-bow and become a bald-headed angel ere its time, Providence has decreed that it should never, never blow its little nose. Notwithstanding the defect, I love it.

There was no business in Osaka that day because of the sunshine and the budding of the trees. Everybody went to a tea-house with his friends. I went also, but first ran along a boulevard by the side of the river, pre tending to look at the Mint. This was only a common place of solid granite where they turn out dollars and rubbish of that kind. All along the boulevard the cherry, peach, and plum trees, pink, white, and red, touched branches and made a belt of velvety soft colour as far as the eye could reach. Weeping willows were the normal ornaments of the waterside, this revel of bloom being only part of the prodigality of Spring. The Mint may make a hundred thousand dollars a day, but all the silver in its keeping will not bring again the three weeks of the peach blossom which, even beyond the chrysanthemum, is the crown and glory of Japan. For some act of surpassing merit performed in a past life I have been enabled to hit those three weeks in the middle.

"Now is the Japanese festival of the cherry blossom," said the guide. "All the people will be festive. They will pray too and go to the tea-gardens."

Now you might wall an Englishman about with cherry trees in bloom from head to heel, and after the first day he would begin to complain of the smell. As you know, the Japanese arrange a good many of their festivals in honour of flowers, and this is surely commendable, for blossoms are the most tolerant of gods.

The tea-house system of the Japanese filled me with pleasure at a pleasure that I could not fully comprehend. It pays a company in Osaka to build on the outskirts of the town a nine-storied pagoda of wood and iron, to lay out elaborate gardens round it, and to hang the whole with strings of blood-red lanterns, because the Japanese will come wherever there is a good view to sit on a mat and discuss tea and sweetmeats and *saki*. This Eiffel Tower is, to tell the truth, anything but pretty, yet the surroundings redeem it. Although it was not quite completed, the lower storeys were full of tea-stalls and tea-drinkers. The men and women were obviously admiring the view. It is an astounding thing to see an Oriental so engaged; it is as though he had stolen something from a sahib.

From Osaka — canal-cut, muddy, and fascinating Osaka — the Professor, Mister Yamagutchi, — the guide, — and I took train to Kioto, an hour from Osaka. On the road I saw four buffaloes at as many rice-ploughs — which was noticeable as well as wasteful. A buffalo at rest must cover the half of a Japanese field; but perhaps they are kept on the mountain ledges and only pulled down when wanted. The Professor says that what I call buffalo is really bullock. The worst of travelling with an accurate man is his accuracy. We argued about the Japanese in the train, about his present and his future, and the manner in which he has ranged himself on the side of the grosser nations of the earth.

"Did it hurt his feelings very much to wear our clothes? Didn't he rebel when he put on a pair of trousers for the first time? Won't he grow sensible some day and drop foreign habits?" These were some of the questions I put to the landscape and the Professor.

"He was a baby," said the latter, "a big baby. I think his sense of humour was at the bottom of the change, but he didn't know that a nation which once wears trousers never takes 'em off. You see 'enlightened' Japan is only one-and-twenty years old, and people are not very wise at one-and-twenty. Read Reed's *Japan* and learn how the change came about. There

was a Mikado and a *Shogun* who was Sir Frederick
Roberts, but he tried to be the Viceroy and — "

"Bother the *Shogun!* I've seen something like the Babu
class, and something like the farmer class. What I want
to see is the Rajput class — the man who used to wear
the thousands and thousands of swords in the curio-
shops. Those swords were as much made for use as
a Rajputana sabre. Where are the men who used
'em? Show me a Samurai."

The Professor answered not a word, but scrutinised
heads on the wayside platforms. "I take it that the
high-arched forehead, club nose, and eyes close together
— the Spanish type — are from Rajput stock, while the
German-faced Jap is the Khattri — the lower class."

Thus we talked of the natures and dispositions of men
we knew nothing about till we had decided (1) that
the painful politeness of the Japanese nation rose from
the habit, dropped only twenty years ago, of extended
and emphatic sword-wearing, even as the Rajput is the
pink of courtesy because his friend goes armed; (2) that
this politeness will disappear in another generation, or
will at least be seriously impaired; (3) that the cultured
Japanese of the English pattern will corrupt and defile
the tastes of his neighbours till (4) Japan altogether
ceases to exist as a separate nation and becomes a but-
ton-hook manufacturing appanage of America; (5) that
these things being so, and sure to happen in two or three
hundred years, the Professor and I were lucky to reach
Japan betimes; and (6) that it was foolish to form theories about the country until we had seen a little of it.

So we came to the city of Kioto in regal sunshine, tempered by a breeze that drove the cherry

blossoms in drifts about the streets. One Japanese town, in the southern provinces at least, is very like another to look at — a grey-black sea of house roofs, speckled with the white walls of the fire-proof godowns where merchants and rich men keep their chief treasures. The general level is broken by the temple roofs, which are turned up at the edges, and remotely resemble so many terai-hats. Kioto fills a plain almost entirely surrounded by wooded hills, very familiar in their aspect to those who have seen the Siwaliks. Once upon a time it was the capital of Japan, and to-day numbers two hundred and fifty thousand people. It is laid out like an American town. All the streets run at right angles to each other. That, by the way, is exactly what the Professor and I are doing. We are elaborating the theory of the Japanese people, and we can't agree.

No. XV

KIOTO AND HOW I FELL IN LOVE WITH THE CHIEF
BELLE THERE AFTER I HAD CONFERRED WITH CERTAIN
CHINA MERCHANTS WHO TRAFFICKED IN TEA. SHOWS
FURTHER HOW, IN A GREAT TEMPLE, I BROKE THE
TENTH COMMANDMENT IN FIFTY-THREE PLACES AND
BOWED DOWN BEFORE KANO AND A CARPENTER. TAKES
ME TO ARASHIMA.

> " Could I but write the things I see,
>   My world would haste to gaze with me.
>   But since the traitor Pen hath failed
>   To paint earth's loveliness unveiled,
>   I can but pray my folk who read : —
>   ' For lavish Will take starveling Deed.' "

WE are consorting with sixty of the *Sahib-log* in
the quaintest hotel that ever you saw. It stands on
the hillside overlooking the whole town of Kioto,
and its garden is veritable Japanese. Fantastically
trimmed tea trees, junipers, dwarfed pine, and cherry,
are mixed up with ponds of goldfish, stone lanterns,
quaint rock-work, and velvety turf all at an angle
of thirty-five degrees. Behind us the pines, red and
black, cover the hill and run down in a long spur to
the town. But an auctioneer's catalogue cannot describe
the charms of the place or deal justly with the tea-garden
full of cherry trees that lies a hundred yards below the

hotel. We were solemnly assured that hardly any one came to Kioto. That is why we meet every soul in the ship that had brought us to Nagasaki; and that is why our ears are constantly assailed with the clamour of people who are discussing places which must be "done." An Englishman is a very horrible person when he is on the war-path; so is an American, a Frenchman, or a German.

I had been watching the afternoon sunlight upon the trees and the town, the shift and play of colour in the crowded street of the cherry, and crooning to myself because the sky was blue and I was alive beneath it with a pair of eyes in my head.

Immediately the sun went down behind the hills the air became bitterly cold, but the people in crêpe sashes and silk coats never ceased their sober frolicking. There was to be a great service in honour of the cherry blossom the next day at the chief temple of Kioto, and they were getting ready for it. As the light died in a wash of crimson, the last thing I saw was a frieze of three little Japanese babies with fuzzy top-knots and huge sashes trying to hang head downwards from a bamboo rail. They did it, and the closing eye of day regarded them solemnly as it shut. The effect in *silhouette* was immense!

A company of China tea-merchants were gathered in the smoking-room after dinner, and by consequence talked their own "shop," which was interesting. Their language is not Our language, for they know nothing of the tea-gardens, of drying and withering and rolling, of the assistant who breaks his collar-bone in the middle of the busiest season, or of the sickness that smites the coolie lines at about the same time. They are happy men who get their tea by the break of a thousand chests from the interior of the country and play with it upon the London markets. None the less they have a very wholesome respect for Indian tea, which they cordially detest. Here is the sort of argument that a Foochow man, himself a very heavy buyer, flung at me across the table.

"You may talk about your Indian teas, — Assam and Kangra, or whatever you call them, — but I tell *you* that if ever they get a strong hold in England, the doctors will be down on them, Sir. They'll be medically forbidden. See if they aren't. They shatter your nerves to pieces. Unfit for human consumption — that's what they are. Though I don't deny they *are* selling at Home. They don't keep, though. After three months, the sorts that I've seen in London turn to hay."

"I think you are wrong there," said a Hankow man. "My experience is that the Indian teas keep better than ours by a long way. But" — turning to me — "if we could only get the China Government to take off the duties, we could smash Indian tea and every one connected with it. We could lay down tea in Mincing Lane at threepence a pound. No, we do not adulterate our teas. That's one of *your* tricks in India. We get it as pure as yours — every chest in the break equal to sample."

"You can trust your native buyers then?" I interrupted.

"Trust 'em? Of course we can," cut in the Foochow merchant. "There are no tea-gardens in China as you understand them. The peasantry cultivate the tea, and the buyers buy from them for cash each season. You can

give a Chinaman a hundred thousand dollars and tell him
to turn it into tea of your own particular chop — up
to sample. Of course the man may be a thorough-paced
rogue in many ways, but he knows better than to play
the fool with an English house. Back comes your tea
— a thousand half-chests, we'll say. You open perhaps
five, and the balance go home untried. But they are all
equal to sample. That's business, that is. The Chinaman's a born merchant and full of backbone. I like him
for business purposes. The Jap's no use. He isn't man
enough to handle a hundred thousand dollars. Very
possibly he'd run off with it — or try to."

"The Jap has no business savvy. God knows I hate
the Chinamen," said a bass voice behind the tobacco
smoke, " but you can do business with him. The Jap's
a little huckster who can't see beyond his nose."

They called for drinks and told tales, these merchants
of China, — tales of money and bales and boxes, — but
through all their stories there was an implied leaning
upon native help which, even allowing for the peculiari-
ties of China, was rather startling. " The compradore
did this: Ho Whang did that: a syndicate of Pekin
bankers did the other thing" — and so on. I wondered
whether a certain lordly indifference as to details had
anything to do with eccentricities in the China tea-
breaks and fluctuations of quality, which do occur in
spite of all the men said to the contrary. Again, the
merchants spoke of China as a place where fortunes are
made — a land only waiting to be opened up to pay a
hundredfold. They told me of the Home Government
helping private trade, in kind and unobtrusive ways, to get
a firmer hold on the Public Works Department contracts

that are now flying abroad. This was pleasant hearing.
But the strangest thing of all was the tone of hope and
almost contentment that pervaded their speech. They
were well-to-do men making money, and they liked their
lives. You know how, when two or three of Us are
gathered together in our own barren pauper land, we
groan in chorus and are disconsolate. The civilian, the
military man, and the merchant, they are all alike. The
one overworked and broken by exchange, the second a
highly organised beggar, and the third a nobody in
particular, always at loggerheads with what he con-
siders an academical Government. I knew in a way
that We were a grim and miserable community in
India, but I did not know the measure of Our fall till
I heard men talking about fortunes, success, money, and
the pleasure, good living, and frequent trips to England
that money brings. Their friends did not seem to die
with unnatural swiftness, and their wealth enabled them
to endure the calamity of Exchange with calm. Yes, we
of India are a wretched folk.

Very early in the dawn, before the nesting sparrows
were awake, there was a sound in the air which frightened me out of my virtuous sleep. It was a lisping
mutter — very deep and entirely strange. "That's an
earthquake, and the hillside is beginning to slide," quoth
I, taking measures of defence. The sound repeated
itself again and again, till I argued, that if it were the
precursor of an earthquake, the affair had stuck half-
way. At breakfast men said: "That was the great
bell of Kioto just next door to the hotel a little
way up the hillside. As a bell, y'know, it's rather a
failure, from an English point of view. They don't

ring it properly, and the volume of sound is comparatively insignificant."

"So I fancied when I first heard it," I said casually,
and went out up the hill under sunshine that filled the
heart and trees, that filled the eye with joy. You know
the unadulterated pleasure of that first clear morning
in the Hills when a month's solid idleness lies before
the loafer, and the scent of the deodars mixes with the
scent of the meditative cigar. That was my portion
when I stepped through the violet-studded long grass into
forgotten little Japanese cemeteries — all broken pillars
and lichened tablets — till I found, under a cut in the
hillside, the big bell of Kioto — twenty feet of green
bronze hung inside a fantastically roofed shed of wooden
beams. A beam, by the way, *is* a beam in Japan; anything under a foot thick is a stick. These beams were
the best parts of big trees, clamped with bronze and iron
A knuckle rapped lightly on the lip of the bell — it was
not more than five feet from the ground — made the great
monster breathe heavily, and the blow of a stick started
a hundred shrill-voiced echoes round the darkness of its
dome. At one side, guyed by half a dozen small hawsers,
hung a battering-ram, a twelve-foot spar bound with iron,
its nose pointing full-butt at a chrysanthemum in high
relief on the belly of the bell. Then, by special favour
of Providence, which always looks after the idle, they
began to sound sixty strokes. Half a dozen men swung
the ram back and forth with shoutings and outcries, till
it had gathered sufficient way, and the loosened ropes
let it hurl itself against the chrysanthemum. The boom
of the smitten bronze was swallowed up by the earth
below and the hillside behind, so that its volume was

not proportionate to the size of the bell, exactly as the men had said. An English ringer would have made thrice as much of it. But then he would have lost the crawling jar that ran through rock-stone and pine for twenty yards round, that beat through the body of the listener and died away under his feet like the shock of a distant blasting. I endured twenty strokes and removed myself, not in the least ashamed of mistaking the sound for an earthquake. Many times since I have heard the bell speak when I was far off. It says *B-r-r-r* very deep down in its throat, but when you have once caught the noise you will never forget it. And so much for the big bell of Kioto.

From its house a staircase of cut stone takes you down to the temple of Chion-in, where I arrived on Easter Sunday just before service, and in time to see the procession of the Cherry Blossom. They had a special service at a place called St. Peter's at Rome about the same time, but the priests of Buddha excelled the priests of the Pope. Thus it happened. The main front of the temple was three hundred feet long, a hundred feet deep, and sixty feet high. One roof covered it all, and saving for the tiles there was no stone in the structure; nothing but wood three hundred years old, as hard as iron. The pillars that upheld the roof were three feet, four feet, and five feet in diameter, and guiltless of any paint. They showed the natural grain of the wood till they were lost in the rich brown darkness far overhead. The cross-beams were of grained wood of great richness; cedar-wood and camphor-wood and the hearts of gigantic pine had been put under requisition for the great work. One carpenter — they call him only a carpenter — had designed the whole, and his name is remembered to this day. A half of the temple was railed off for the congregation by a two-foot railing, over which silks of ancient device had been thrown. Within the railing were all the religious fittings, but these I cannot describe. All I remember was row upon row of little lacquered stands each holding a rolled volume of sacred writings; an altar as tall as a cathedral organ where gold strove with colour, colour with lacquer, and lacquer with inlay, and candles such as Holy Mother Church uses only on her greatest days, shed a yellow light that softened all. Bronze incense-burners in the likeness of dragons and devils fumed under the shadow of silken banners, behind which, wood tracery, as delicate as frost on a window-pane, climbed to the ridge-pole. Only there was no visible roof to this temple. The light faded away under the monstrous beams, and we might have been in a cave a hundred fathoms below the earth but for the sunshine and blue sky at the portals, where the little children squabbled and shouted.

On my word, I tried to note down soberly what lay before me, but the eye tired, and the pencil ran off into fragmentary ejaculations. But what would you have done if you had seen what I saw when I went round the temple verandah to what we must call a vestry at the back ? It was a big building connected with the main one by a wooden bridge of deepest time-worn brown. Down the bridge ran a line of saffron-coloured matting, and down the matting, very slowly and solemnly, as befitted their high office, filed three and fifty priests, each one clad in at least four garments of brocade, crêpe, and silk. There were silks that do not see the light of the markets, and brocades that only temple wardrobes know.

There was sea-green watered silk with golden dragons; terra-cotta crêpe with ivory-white chrysanthemums clustering upon it; black-barred silk shot with yellow flames; lapis-lazuli silk and silver fishes; avanturine silk with plaques of grey-green let in; cloth of gold over dragon's blood; and saffron and brown silk stiff as a board with embroidery. We returned to the temple now filled with the gorgeous robes. The little lacquer stands were the priests' book-racks. Some lay down among them, while others moved very softly about the golden altars and the incense-burners; and the high priest disposed himself, with his back to the congregation, in a golden chair through which his robe winked like the shards of a tiger-beetle.

In solemn calm the books were unrolled, and the priests began chanting Pali texts in honour of the Apostle of Unworldliness, who had written that they were not to wear gold or mixed colours, or touch the precious metals. But for a few unimportant accessories in the way of half-seen images of great men — but these could have been called saints — the scene before me might have been unrolled in a Roman Catholic cathedral, say the rich one at Arundel. The same thought was in other minds, for in a pause of the slow chant a voice behind me whispered: —

> "To hear the blessed mutter of the mass
> And see God made and eaten all day long."

It was a man from Hong-Kong, very angry that he too had not been permitted to photograph an interior. He

called all this splendour of ritual and paraphernalia
just "an interior," and revenged himself by spitting
Browning at it.

The chant quickened as the service drew to an end,
and the candles burned low.

We went away to other parts of the temple pursued by
the chorus of the devout till we were out of earshot in a
paradise of screens.   Two or three hundred years ago
there lived a painterman of the name of Kano.   Him the
temple of Chion-in brought to beautify the walls of the
rooms.   Since a wall is a screen, and a screen is a wall,
Kano, R. A., had rather a large job.   But he was helped
by pupils and imitators, and in the end left a few hundred screens which are all finished pictures.   As you
already know, the interior of a temple is very simple in
its arrangements.   The priests live on white mats, in
little rooms, with brown ceilings, that can at pleasure be
thrown into one large room.   This also was the arrangement at Chion-in, though the rooms were comparatively
large and gave on to sumptuous verandahs and passages.   Since the Emperor occasionally visited the place
there was a room set apart for him of more than ordinary splendour.   Twisted silk tassels of intricate design
served in lieu of catches to pull back the sliding screens,
and the woodwork was lacquered.   These be only feeble
words, but it is not in my grip to express the restfulness
of it all, or the power that knew how to secure the
desired effect with a turn of the wrist.   The great Kano
drew numbed pheasants huddled together on the snow-
covered bough of a pine; or a peacock in his pride
spreading his tail to delight his womenfolk; or a riot of
chrysanthemums poured out of a vase; or the figures of

toilworn countryfolk coming home from market; or a hunting scene at the foot of Fujiyama. The equally great carpenter who built the temple framed each picture with absolute precision under a ceiling that was a miracle of device, and Time, the greatest artist of the three, touched the gold so that it became amber, and the woodwork so that it grew dark honey-colour, and the shining surface of the lacquer so that it became deep and rich and semi-transparent. As in one room, so in all the others. Sometimes we slid back the screens and discovered a tiny bald-pated acolyte praying over an incense-burner, and sometimes a lean priest eating his rice; but generally the rooms were empty, swept and garnished.

Minor artists had worked with Kano the magnificent. These had been allowed to lay brush upon panels of wood in the outer verandahs, and very faithfully had they toiled. It was not till the guide called my atten-tion to them that I discovered scores of sketches in monochrome low down on the verandah doors. An iris broken by the fall of a branch torn off by a surly ape; a bamboo spray bowed before the wind that was ruffling a lake; a warrior of the past ambushing his enemy in a thicket, hand on sword, and mouth gathered into puckers of intensest concentration, were among the many notes that met my eye. How long, think you, would a sepia-drawing stand without defacement in the midst of our civilisation were it put on the bottom panel of a door, or the scantling of a kitchen passage? Yet in this gentle country a man may stoop down and write his name in the very dust, certain that, if the writing be craftily done, his children's children will reverently let it stand

"Of course there are no such temples made nowadays," I said, when we regained the sunshine, and the Professor was trying to find out how panel pictures and paper screens went so well with the dark dignity of massive woodwork.

"They are building a temple on the other side of the city," said Mister Yamagutchi. "Come along, and see the hair-ropes which hang there."

We came flying in our 'rickshaws across Kioto, till we saw netted in a hundred cobwebs of scaffolding a temple even larger than the great Chion-in.

"That was burned down long ago, — the old temple that was here, you know. Then the people made a penny subscription from all parts of Japan, and those who could not send money sent their hair to be made into rope. They have been ten years building this new temple. It is all wood," said the guide.

The place was alive with men who were putting the finishing touches to the great tiled roof and laying down the floors. Wooden pillars as gigantic, carving as wantonly elaborate, eaves as intricate in their mouldings, and joinery as perfect as anything in the Chion-in temple met me at every turn. But the fresh-cut wood was creamy white and lemon where, in the older building, it had been iron-hard and brown. Only the raw ends of the joists were stopped with white lacquer to prevent the incursions of insects, and the deeper tracery was protected against birds by fine wire netting. Everything else was wood — wood down to the massive clamped and bolted beams of the foundation which I investigated through gaps in the flooring.

Japan is a great people. Her masons play with stone,

her carpenters with wood, her smiths with iron, and her artists with life, death, and all the eye can take in. Mercifully she has been denied the last touch of firmness in her character which would enable her to play with the whole round world. We possess that — We, the nation of the glass flower-shade, the pink worsted mat, the red and green china puppy-dog, and the poisonous Brussels carpet. It is our compensation. . . .

"Temples!" said a man from Calcutta, some hours later as I raved about what I had seen. "Temples! I'm sick of temples. If I've seen one, I've seen fifty thou-sand of 'em — all exactly alike. But I tell you what is exciting. Go down the rapids at Arashima, — eight miles from here. It's better fun than any temple with a fat-faced Buddha in the middle."

But I took my friend's advice. Have I managed to convey the impression that April is fine in Japan? Then I apologise. It is generally rainy, and the rain is cold; but the sunshine when it comes is worth it all. We shouted with joy of living when our fiery, untamed 'rickshaws bounded from stone to stone of the vilely paved streets of the suburbs and brought us into what ought to have been vegetable gardens but were called fields. The face of the flat lands was cut up in every direction by bunds, and all the roads seem to run on the top of them.

"Never," said the Professor, driving his stick into the black soil, "never have I imagined irrigation so perfectly controlled as this is. Look at the *rajbahars* faced with stone and fitted with sluices; look at the water-wheels and, — phew! but they manure their fields too well."

The first circle of fields round any town is always

pretty rank, but this superfluity of scent continued throughout the country. Saving a few parts near Dacca and Patna, the face of the land was more thickly populated than Bengal and was worked five times better. There was no single patch untilled, and no cultivation that was not up to the full limit of the soil's productiveness. Onions, barley, in little ridges between the ridges of tea, beans, rice, and a half a dozen other things that we did not know the names of, crowded the eye already wearied with the glare of the golden mustard. Manure is a good thing, but manual labour is better. We saw both even to excess. When a Japanese ryot has done everything to his field that he can possibly think of, he weeds the barley stalk by stalk with his finger and thumb. This is true. I saw a man doing it.

We headed through the marvellous country straight across the plain on which Kioto stands, till we reached the range of hills on the far side, and found ourselves mixed up with half a mile of lumber-yard.

Cultivation and water-cuts were gone, and our tireless 'rickshaws were running by the side of a broad, shallow river, choked with logs of every size. I am prepared to believe anything of the Japanese, but I do not see why Nature, which they say is the same pitiless Power all the world over, should send them their logs unsplintered by rocks, neatly barked, and with a slot neatly cut at the end of each pole for the reception of a rope. I have seen timber fly down the Ravi in spate, and it was hooked out as ragged as a tooth-brush. This material comes down clean. Consequently the slot is another miracle.

"When the day is fine," said the guide, softly, "all the people of Kioto come to Arashima to have picnics."

"But they are always having picnics in the cherry-tree gardens. They picnic in the tea-houses. They — they — "

" Yes, when it is a fine day, they always go somewhere and picnic."

"But why? Man isn't made to picnic."

"But why? Because it is a fine day. Englishmen say that the money of the Japanese comes from heaven, because they always do nothing — so you think. But look now, here is a pretty place."

The river charged down a turn in the pine-grown hills, and broke in silver upon the timber and the remains of a light bridge washed away some days before. On our side, and arranged so as to face the fairest view of the young maples, stood a row of tea-houses and booths built over the stream. The sunlight that could not soften the gloom of the pines dwelt tenderly among the green of the maples and touched the reaches below where the cherry blossom broke in pink foam against the black-roofed houses of a village across the water.

There I stopped.

No. XVI

THE PARTY IN THE PARLOUR WHO PLAYED GAMES. A
COMPLETE HISTORY OF ALL MODERN JAPANESE ART;
A SURVEY OF THE PAST, AND A PROPHECY OF THE
FUTURE, ARRANGED AND COMPOSED IN THE KIOTO
FACTORIES.

> "Oh, brave new world that has such creatures in it,
> How beautiful mankind is ! "

How I got to the tea-house I cannot tell. Perhaps a
pretty girl waved a bough of cherry blossom at me, and
I followed the invitation. I know that I sprawled upon
the mats and watched the clouds scudding across the hills
and the logs flying down the rapids, and smelt the smell
of the raw peeled timber, and listened to the grunts of
the boatmen as they wrestled with that and the rush
of the river, and was altogether happier than it is lawful
for a man to be.

The lady of the tea-house insisted upon screening us
off from the other pleasure-parties who were tiffining in
the same verandah. She brought beautiful blue screens
with storks on them and slid them into grooves. I stood
it as long as I could. There were peals of laughter
in the next compartment, the pattering of soft feet, the
clinking of little dishes, and at the chinks of the screens
the twinkle of diamond eyes. A whole family had come
in from Kioto for the day's pleasuring. Mamma looked

after grandmamma, and the young aunt looked after a guitar, and the two girls of fourteen and fifteen looked after a merry little tomboy of eight, who, when she thought of it, looked after the baby who had the air of looking after the whole party. Grandmamma was dressed in dark blue, mamma in blue and grey, the girls had gorgeous dresses of lilac, fawn, and primrose crêpe with silk sashes, the colour of apple blossom and the inside of a newly cut melon; the tomboy was in old gold and russet brown; but the baby tumbled his fat little body across the floor among the dishes in the colours of the Japanese rainbow, which owns no crude tints. They were all pretty, all except grandmamma, who was merely good-humoured and very bald, and when they had finished their dainty dinner, and the brown lanquer stands, the blue and white crockery, and the jade-green drinking-cups had been taken away, the aunt played a little piece on the *samisen*, and the girls played blindman's-buff all round the tiny room.

Flesh and blood could not have stayed on the other side of the screens. I wanted to play too, but I was too big and too rough, and so could only sit in the verandah, watching these dainty bits of Dresden at their game. They shrieked and giggled and chattered and sat down on the floor with the innocent abandon of maidenhood, and broke off to kiss the baby when he showed signs of being overlooked. They played puss-in-the-corner, their feet tied with blue and white handkerchiefs because the room did not allow unfettered freedom of limb, and when they could play no more for laughing, they fanned themselves as they lay propped up against the blue screens,—each girl a picture no painter could

2 a

reproduce, — and I shrieked with the best of them till I rolled off the verandah and nearly dropped into the laughing street. Was I a fool? Then I fooled in good company, for an austere man from India — a person who puts his faith in race-horses and believes nothing except the Civil Code — was also at Arashima that day. I met him flushed and excited.

"'Had a lively time," he panted, with a hundred children at his heels. "There's a sort of roulette table here where you can gamble for cakes. I bought the owner's stock-in-trade for three dollars and ran the Monte Carlo for the benefit of the kids — about five thousand of 'em. Never had such fun in my life. It beats the Simla lotteries hollow. They were perfectly orderly till they had cleared the tables of everything except a big sugar-tortoise. Then they rushed the bank, and I ran away."

And he was a hard man who had not played with anything as innocent as sweetmeats for many years!

When we were all weak with laughing, and the Professor's camera was mixed up in a tangle of laughing maidens to the confusion of his pictures, we too ran away from the tea-house and wandered down the river bank till we found a boat of sewn planks which poled us across the swollen river, and landed us on a little rocky path overhanging the water where the iris and the violet ran riot together and jubilant waterfalls raced through the undergrowth of pine and maple. We were at the foot of the Arashima rapids, and all the pretty girls of Kioto were with us looking at the view. Up-stream a lonely black pine stood out from all its fellows to peer up the bend where the racing water ran deep in oily swirls. Down-stream the river threshed across the rocks and troubled the fields of fresh logs on its bosom, while men in blue drove silver-white boats gunwale-deep into the foam of its onset and hooked the logs away. Underfoot the rich earth of the hillside sent up the breath of the turn of the year to the maples that had already caught the message from the fire-winds of April. Oh! it was good to be alive, to trample the stalks of the iris, to drag down the cherry-bloom spray in a wash of dew across the face, and to gather the violets for the mere pleasure of heaving them into the torrent and reaching out for fairer flowers.

" What a nuisance it is to be a slave to the camera," said the Professor, upon whom the dumb influences of the season were working though he knew it not.

" What a nuisance it is to be a slave to the pen," I answered, for the spring had come to the land. I had hated the spring for seven years because to me it meant discomfort.

" Let us go straight home and see the flowers come out in the Parks."

" Let us enjoy what lies to our hand, you Philistine." And we did till a cloud darkened and a wind ruffled the river reaches, and we returned to our 'rickshaws sighing with contentment.

" How many people do you suppose the land supports to the square mile ? " said the Professor, at a turn in the homeward road. He had been reading statistics.

" Nine hundred," I said at a venture. " It's thicker set with humans than Sarun or Behar. Say one thousand."

" Two thousand two hundred and fifty odd. Can you believe it ? "

" Looking at the landscape I can, but I don't suppose India will believe it. S'pose I write fifteen hundred ? "

" They'll say you exaggerate just the same. Better stick to the true total. Two thousand two hundred and fifty-six to the square mile, and not a sign of poverty in the houses. How do they do it ? "

I should like to know the answer to that question. Japan of my limited view is inhabited almost entirely by little children whose duty is to prevent their elders from becoming too frivolous. The babies do a little work occasionally, but their parents interfere by petting them. At Yami's hotel the attendance is in the hands of ten-year-olds because everybody else has gone out picnicing among the cherry trees. The little imps find time to do a man's work and to scuffle on the staircase between whiles. My special servitor, called " The Bishop " on account of the gravity of his appearance, his blue apron, and gaiters, is the liveliest of the lot, but even his energy cannot account for the Professor's statistics of population. . . .

I have seen one sort of work among the Japanese, but it was not the kind that makes crops. It was purely artistic. A ward of the city of Kioto is devoted to manufactures. A manufacturer in this part of the world does not hang out a sign. He may be known in Paris and New York : that is the concern of the two cities. The Englishman who wishes to find his establishment in Kioto has to hunt for him up and down slums with the aid of a guide. I have seen three manufactories. The first was of porcelain-ware, the second of *cloissonnée,* and the third of lacquer, inlay, and bronzes. The first was behind black wooden palings, and for external appearance might just

as well have been a tripe-shop.   Inside sat the manager
opposite a tiny garden four feet square in which a
papery-looking palm grew out of a coarse stoneware pot
and overshadowed a dwarfed pine.   The rest of the
room was filled with pottery waiting to be packed —
modern Satsuma for the most part, the sort of thing you
get at an auction.

"This made send Europe — India — America," said the
manager, calmly.   "You come to see ?"

He took us along a verandah of polished wood to the
kilns, to the clay vats, and the yards where the tiny
"saggers" were awaiting their complement of pottery.
There are differences many and technical between Japanese and Burslem pottery in the making, but these are
of no consequence.   In the moulding house, where they
were making the bodies of Satsuma vases, the wheels, all
worked by hand, ran true as a hair.   The potter sat on a
clean mat with his tea-things at his side.   When he had
turned out a vase-body he saw that it was good, nodded
appreciatively to himself, and poured out some tea ere
starting the next one.   The potters lived close to the
kilns and had nothing pretty to look at.   It was dif
ferent in the painting rooms.   Here in a cabinet-like
house sat the men, women, and boys who painted the
designs on the vases after the first firing.   That all their
arrangements were scrupulously neat is only saying that
they were Japanese; that their surroundings were fair
and proper is only saying that they were artists.   A sprig
of a cherry blossom stood out defiantly against the black
of the garden paling; a gnarled pine cut the blue of the
sky with its spiky splinters as it lifted itself above the
paling, and in a little pond the iris and the horsetail

nodded to the wind. The workers when at fault had only to lift their eyes, and Nature herself would graciously supply the missing link of a design. Somewhere in dirty England men dream of craftsmen working under conditions which shall help and not stifle the half-formed thought. They even form guilds and write semi-rhythmical prayers to Time and Chance and all the other gods that they worship, to bring about the desired end. Would they have their dream realised, let them see how they make pottery in Japan, each man sitting on a snowy mat with loveliness of line and colour within arm's length of him, while with downcast eyes he — splashes in the conventional diaper of a Satsuma vase as fast as he can! The Barbarians want Satsuma and they shall have it, if it has to be made in Kioto one piece per twenty minutes. So much for the baser forms of the craft!

The owner of the second establishment lived in a blackwood cabinet — it was profanation to call it a house — alone with a bronze of priceless workmanship, a set of blackwood furniture, and all the medals that his work had won for him in England, France, Germany, and America. He was a very quiet and cat-like man, and spoke almost in a whisper. Would we be pleased to inspect the manufactory? He led us through a garden — it was nothing in his eyes, but we stopped to admire long. Stone lanterns, green with moss, peeped through clumps of papery bamboos where bronze storks were pretending to feed. A dwarfed pine, its foliage trimmed to dish-like plaques, threw its arms far across a fairy pond where the fat, lazy carp grubbed and rooted, and a couple of eared grebes squawked at us from the protection of the

— waterbutt. So perfect was the silence of the place that we heard the cherry blossoms falling into the water and the lisping of the fish against the stones. We were in the very heart of the Willow-Pattern Plate and loath to move for fear of breaking it. The Japanese are born bower-birds. They collect water-worn stones, quaintly shaped rocks, and veined pebbles for the ornamentation of their homes. When they shift house they take the garden away with them — pine trees and all — and the incoming tenant has a free hand.

Half a dozen steps took us over the path of mossy stones to a house where the whole manufactory was at work. One room held the enamel powders all neatly arranged in jars of scrupulous cleanliness, a few blank copper vases ready to be operated on, an invisible bird who whistled and whooped in his cage, and a case of gaily painted butterflies ready for reference when patterns were wanted. In the next room sat the manufactory — three men, five women, and two boys — all as silent as sleep. It is one thing to read of *cloissonnée* making, but quite another to watch it being made. I began to understand the cost of the ware when I saw a man working out a pattern of sprigs and butterflies on a plate about ten inches in diameter. With finest silver ribbon wire, set on edge, less than the sixteenth of an inch high, he followed the curves of the drawing at his side, pinching the wire into tendrils and the serrated outlines of leaves with infinite patience. A rough touch on the raw copper-plate would have sent the pattern flying into a thousand disconnected threads. When all was put down on the copper, the plate would be warmed just sufficiently to allow the wires to stick firmly to the copper, the pattern then showing in raised lines. Followed the colouring, which was done by little boys in spectacles. With a pair of tiniest steel chopsticks they filled from bowls at their sides each compartment of the pattern with its proper hue of paste. There is not much room allowed for error in filling the spots on a butterfly's wing with avanturine enamel when the said wings are less than an inch across. I watched the delicate play of wrist and hand till I was wearied, and the manager showed me his patterns — terrible dragons, clustered chrysanthemums, butterflies, and diapers as fine as frost on a window-pane — all drawn in unerring line. "Those things are our subjects. I compile from them, and when I want some new colours I go and look at those dead butterflies," said he. After the enamel has been filled in, the pot or plate goes to be fired, and the enamel bubbles all over the boundary lines of wires, and the whole comes from the furnace looking like delicate majolica. It may take a month to put a pattern on the plate in outline, another month to fill in the enamel, but the real expenditure of time does not commence till the polishing. A man sits down with the rough article, all his tea-things, a tub of water, a flannel, and two or three saucers full of assorted pebbles from the brook. He does not get a wheel with tripoli, or emery, or buff. He sits down and rubs. He rubs for a month, three months, or a year. He rubs lovingly, with his soul in his finger ends, and little by little the efflorescence of the fired enamel gives way, and he comes down to the lines of silver, and the pattern in all its glory is there waiting for him. I saw a man who had only been a month over the polishing of one little vase five inches high. He would go on for

two months. When I am in America he will be rubbing
still, and the ruby-coloured dragon that romped on a field
of lazuli, each tiny scale and whisker a separate compartment of enamel, will be growing more lovely.

"There is also cheap *cloissonnée* to be bought," said the
manager, with a smile. "We cannot make that. The
vase will be seventy dollars."

I respected him for saying "cannot" instead of "do
not." There spoke the artist.

Our last visit was paid to the largest establishment in
Kioto, where boys made gold inlay on iron, sitting in
camphor-wood verandahs overlooking a garden lovelier
than any that had gone before. They had been caught
young, even as is the custom in India. A real grown-up
man was employed on the horrible story, in iron, gold,
and silver, of two priests who waked up a Rain-dragon
and had to run for it, all round the edge of a big shield;
but the liveliest worker of the batch was a small fat baby
who had been given a tenpenny nail, a hammer, and a
block of metal to play with, that he might soak in the
art by which he would live, through the pores of his skin.
He crowed and chuckled as he whacked. There are not
many five-year-olds in England who could hammer anything without pulping their little pink fingers. The
baby had learned how to hit straight. On the wall of
the room hung a Japanese painting of the Apotheosis
of Art. It represented with fidelity all the processes of
pottery from the digging of the clay to the last firing.
But all the pencilled scorn of the artist was reserved for
the closing scene, where an Englishman, his arm round
his wife's waist, was inspecting a shop full of curios.
The Japanese are not impressed with the grace of our

clothing or the beauty of our countenances. Later we beheld the manufacture of gold lacquer, which is laid on speck by speck from an agate palette fitted on the artist's thumb; and the carving of ivory, which is exciting until you begin to realise that the graver never slips.

" A lot of their art is purely mechanical " said the Professor, when he was safe back in the hotel.

" So's a lot of ours — 'specially our pictures. Only we can't be spiritedly mechanical," I answered. " Fancy a people like the Japanese solemnly going in for a constitution. Observe! The only two nations with constitution worth having are the English and the Americans. The English can only be artistic in spots and by way of the art of other nations — Sicilian tapestries, Persian saddle-bags, Khoten carpets, and the sweepings of pawnbrokers' shops. The Americans are artistic so long as a few of 'em can buy their Art to keep abreast of the times with. Spain is artistic, but she is also disturbed at intervals; France is artistic, but she must have her revolution every twenty years for the sake of fresh material; Russia is artistic, but she occasionally wishes to kill her Czar, and has no sort of Government; Germany is not artistic, because she experienced religion; and Italy is artistic, because she did very badly. India — "

" When you have finished your verdict on the world, perhaps you'll go to bed."

" Consequently," I continued, with scorn, " I am of opinion that a constitution is the worst thing in the world for a people who are blessed with souls above the average. Now the first demand of the artistic temperament is mundane uncertainty. The second is — "

" Sleep," said the Professor, and left the room.

OF THE NATURE OF THE TOKAIDO AND JAPANESE RAIL-
WAY CONSTRUCTION.   ONE TRAVELLER EXPLAINS THE
LIFE OF THE SAHIB-LOG, AND ANOTHER THE ORIGIN OF
DICE.   OF THE BABIES IN THE BATH TUB AND THE
MAN IN D. T.

" When I went to Hell I spoke to the man on the road."
— *Old Saw.*

YOU know the story of the miner who borrowed a dic-
tionary and returned it with the remark that the stories,
though interesting in the main, were too various.   I have
the same complaint to make against Japanese scenery —
twelve hours of it by train from Nagoya to Yokohama.
About seven hundred years ago the king of those days
built a sea-road which he called the Tokaido (or else all
the sea-coast was called the Tokaido, but it's of no importance), which road endures to the present.   Later on,
when the English engineer appeared, he followed the
Grand Trunk more or less closely, and the result has
been a railway that any nation might take off their hat
to.   The last section of the through line from Kioto to
Yokohama was only opened five days before the Professor and I honoured it with an unofficial inspection.

The accommodation of all kinds is arranged for the
benefit of the Japanese; and this is distressing to the
foreigner, who expects in a carriage remotely resembling

E. I. R. rolling-stock the conveniences of that pea-green and very dusty old line. But it suits the Japanese admirably: they hop out at every other station — *pro re nata* — and occasionally get left behind. Two days ago they managed to kill a Government official of high standing between a footboard and a platform, and to-day the Japanese papers are seriously discussing the advantages of lavatories. Far be it from me to interfere with the arrangements of an artistic empire; but for a twelve hours' run there might at least be arrangements.

We had left the close-packed cultivation at the foot of the hills and were running along the shores of a great lake, all steel-blue from one end to the other, except where it was dotted with little islands. Then the lake turned into an arm of the sea, and we ran across it on a cut-stone causeway, and the profligacy of the pines ceased, as the trees had to come down from clothing dank hills, and fight with bowed head, outstretched arms, and firmly planted feet, against the sands of the Pacific, whose breakers were spouting and blowing not a quarter of a mile away from the causeway. The Japs know all about forestry. They stake down wandering sand-torrents, which are still allowed to ruin our crops in the Hoshiarpur district, and they plug a shifting sand-dune with wattle dams and pine seedlings as cleverly as they would pin plank to plank. Were their forest officers trained at Nancy, or are they local products? The stake-binding used to hold the sand is of French pattern, and the diagonal planting out of the trees is also French.

Half a minute after the train dropped this desolate, hardly controlled beach it raced through four or five miles of the suburbs of Patna, but a clean and glorified Patna bowered in bamboo plantations. Then it hit a tunnel and sailed forth into a section of the London, Brighton, and South Coast, or whatever the line is that wants to make the Channel tunnel. At any rate, the embankment was on the beach, and the waves lapped the foot of it, and there was a wall of cut rock to land-ward. Then we disturbed many villages of fishermen, whose verandahs gave on to the track, and whose nets lay almost under our wheels. The railway was still a new thing in that particular part of the world, for mothers held up their babes to see it.

Any one can keep pace with Indian scenery, arranged as it is in reaches of five hundred miles. This blinding alternation of field, mountain, sea-beach, forest, bamboo grove, and rolling moor covered with azalea blossoms was too much for me, so I sought the society of a man who had lived in Japan for twenty years.

"Yes, Japan's an excellent country as regards climate. The rains begin in May or latter April. June, July, and August are hot months. I've known the thermometer as high as 86° at night, but I'd defy the world to produce anything more perfect than the weather between September and May. When one gets seedy, one goes to the hot springs in the Hakone mountains close to Yokohama. There are heaps of places to recruit in, but we English are a healthy lot. Of course we don't have half as much fun as you do in India. We are a small community, and all our amusements are organised by ourselves for our own benefit — concerts, races, and amateur theatricals and the like. You have heaps of 'em in India, haven't you?"

"Oh, yes!" I said, "we enjoy ourselves awfully, 'specially about this time of the year. I quite understand, though, that small communities dependent on themselves for enjoyment are apt to feel a little slow and isolated — almost bored, in fact. But you were saying — ?"

"Well, living is not very dear, and house rent is. A hundred dollars a month gets you a decent house and you can get one for sixty. But house property is down just now in Yokohama. The races are on in Yokohama to-day and Monday. Are you going? No? You ought to go and see all the foreigners enjoying themselves. But I suppose you've seen much better things in India, haven't you? You haven't anything better than old Fuji — Fujiyama. There he is now to the left of the line. What do you think of him?"

I turned and beheld Fujiyama across a sea of upward-sloping fields and woods. It is about fourteen thousand feet high — not very much, according to our ideas. But fourteen thousand feet above the sea when one stands in the midst of sixteen-thousand-foot peaks, is quite another thing from the same height noted at sea-level in a comparatively flat country. The labouring eye crawls up every foot of the dead crater's smooth flank, and at the summit confesses that it has seen nothing in all the Himalayas to match the monster. I was satisfied. Fujiyama was exactly as I had seen it on fans and lacquer boxes; I would not have sold my sight of it for the crest of Kinchinjunga flushed with the morning. Fujiyama is the keynote of Japan. When you understand the one you are in a position to learn something about the other. I tried to get information from my fellow-traveller

" Yes, the Japanese are building railways all over the island. What I mean to say is that the companies are started and financed by Japs, and they make 'em pay. I can't quite tell you where the money comes from, but it's all to be found in the country. Japan's neither rich ᷉or poor, but just comfortable. I'm a merchant myself. ᷉an't say that I altogether like the Jap way o' doing business. You can never be certain whether the little beggar means what he says. Give me a Chinaman to deal with. Other men have told you that, have they? You'll find that opinion at most of the treaty ports. But what I will say is, that the Japanese Government is ᷉bout as enterprising a Government as you could wish, ᷉nd a good one to have dealings with. When Japan has finished reconstructing herself on the new lines, she'll be quite a respectable little Power. See if she isn't. Now we are coming into the Hakone mountains. Watch the railway. It's rather a curiosity."

We came into the Hakone mountains by way of some Irish scenery, a Scotch trout-stream, a Devonshire combe, and an Indian river running masterless over half a mile of pebbles. This was only the prelude to a set of geological illustrations, including the terraces formed by ancient river-beds, denudation, and half a dozen other ations. I was so busy telling the man from Yokohama lies about the height of the Himalayas that I did not watch things closely, till we got to Yokohama, at eight in the evening, and went to the Grand Hotel, where all the clean and nicely dressed people who were just going in to dinner regarded us with scorn, and men, whom we had met on steamers aforetime, dived into photograph books and pretended not to see us. There's a deal of human nature in a man — got up for dinner — when a woman is watching him — and you look like a brick-layer — even in Yokohama.

The Grand is the Semi or Cottage Grand really, but you had better go there unless a friend tells you of a better. A long course of good luck has spoiled me for even average hotels. They are too fine and large at the Grand, and they don't always live up to their grandeur; unlimited electric bells, but no one in particular to answer 'em; printed menu, but the first comers eat all the nice things, and so forth. None the less there are points about the Grand not to be despised. It is modelled on the American fashion, and is but an open door through which you may catch the first gust from the Pacific slope. Officially, there are twice as many English as Americans in the port. Actually, you hear no languages but French, German, or American in the street. My experience is sadly limited, but the American I have heard up to the present, is a tongue as distinct from English as Patagonian.

A gentleman from Boston was kind enough to tell me something about it. He defended the use of "I guess" as a Shakespearian expression to be found in *Richard the Third.* I have learned enough never to argue with a Bostonian.

"All right," I said, "I've never heard a real American say 'I guess'; but what about the balance of your extraordinary tongue? Do you mean to say that it has anything in common with ours except the auxiliary verbs, the name of the Creator, and Damn? Listen to the men at the next table."

"They are Westerners," said the man from Boston.

who should say "observe this cassowary." "They are Westerners, and if you want to make a Westerner mad tell him he is not like an Englishman. They think they are like the English. They are awfully thin-skinned in the West. Now in Boston it's different. We don't care what the English people think of us."

The idea of the English people sitting down to think about Boston, while Boston on the other side of the water ostentatiously "didn't care," made me snigger. The man told me stories. He belonged to a Republic. That was why every man of his acquaintance belonged either "to one of the first families in Boston" or else "was of good Salem stock, and his fathers had come over in the *Mayflower*." I felt as though I were moving in the midst of a novel. Fancy having to explain to the casual stranger the blood and breeding of the hero of every anecdote. I wonder whether many people in Boston are like my friend with the Salem families. I am going there to see.

"There's no romance in America—it's all hard, business facts," said a man from the Pacific slope, after I had expressed my opinion about some rather curious murder cases which might have been called miscarriages of justice. Ten minutes later, I heard him say slowly, *apropos* of a game called "Round the Horn" (this is a bad game. Don't play it with a stranger.) "Well, it's a good thing for this game that Omaha came up. Dice were invented in Omaha, and the man who invented 'em he made a colossal fortune."

I said nothing. I began to feel faint. The man must have noticed it. "Six-and-twenty years ago, Omaha came up," he repeated, looking me in the eye. "and the

2 B

number of dice that have been made in Omaha since that time is incalculable."

"There is no romance in America," I moaned like a stricken ring-dove, in the Professor's ear. "Nothing but hard business facts, and the first families of Boston, Massachusetts, invented dice at Omaha when it first came up, twenty-six years ago, and that's the solid truth. What am I to do with a people like this?"

"Are you describing Japan or America? For goodness' sake, stick to one or the other," said the Professor.

"It wasn't my fault. There's a bit of America in the bar-room, and on my word it's rather more interesting than Japan. Let's go across to 'Frisco and hear some more lies."

"Let's go and look at photographs, and refrain from mixing our countries or our drinks."

By the way, wherever you go in the Further East be humble to the white trader. Recollect that you are only a poor beast of a buyer with a few dirty dollars in your pockets, and you can't expect a man to demean himself by taking them. And observe humility not only in the shops, but elsewhere. I was anxious to know how I should cross the Pacific to 'Frisco, and very foolishly went to an office where they might, under certain circumstances, be supposed to attend to these things. But no anxiety troubled the sprightly soul who happened to be in the office-chair. "There's heaps of time for finding out later on," he said, "and anyhow, I'm going to the races this afternoon. Come later on." I put my head in the spittoon, and crawled out under the door.

When I am left behind by the steamer it will console me to know that that young man had a good time, and

·won heavily. Everybody keeps horses in Yokohama, and the horses are nice little fat little tubs, of the circus persuasion. I didn't go to the races, but a Calcutta man did, and returned saying that "they ran 13–2 cart-horses, and even time for a mile was four minutes and twenty-seven seconds." Perhaps he had lost heavily, but I can vouch for the riding of the few gentlemen I saw outside the animals. It is very impartial and remarkably all round.

Just when the man from Boston was beginning to tell me some more stories about first families, the Professor developed an unholy taste for hot springs, and bore me off to a place called Myanoshita to wash myself. "We'll come back and look at Yokohama later on, but we must go to this because it's so beautiful."

"I'm getting tired of scenery. It's all beautiful and it can't be described, but these men here tell you stories about America. Did you ever hear how the people of Carmel lynched Edward M. Petree for preaching the gospel without making a collection at the end of the service? There's no romance in America — it's all hard business facts. Edward M. Petree was — "

"*Are* you going to see Japan or are you not?"

I went to see. First in a train for one hour in the company of a carriageful of howling Globe-trotters, then in a 'rickshaw for four. You cannot appreciate scenery unless you sit in a 'rickshaw. We struck after seven miles of modified flat — the flattery of Nature that lures you to her more rugged heart — a mountain river all black pools and boiling foam. Him we followed into the hills along a road cut into the crumbling volcanic rock and entirely unmetalled. It was as hard as the Simla cartroad, but those far hills behind Kalka have no such pine and maple, ash and willow. It was a land of green-clothed cliff and silver waterfall, lovely beyond the defilement of the pen. At every turn in the road whence a view could be commanded, stood a little tea-house full of admiring Japanese. The Jap dresses in blue because he knows that it contrasts well with the colour of the pines. When he dies he goes to a heaven of his own because the colouring of ours is too crude to suit him.

We kept the valley of the glorified stream till the waters sank out of sight down the cliff side and we could but hear them calling to one another through the tangle of the trees. Where the woodlands were lovelier, the gorge deepest, and the colours of the young hornbeam most tender, they had clapped down two vile hostelries of wood and glass, and a village that lived by selling turned wood and glass inlay things to the tourist.

Australians, Anglo-Indians, dwellers in London and the parts beyond the Channel were running up and down the slopes of the hotel garden, and by their strange dresses doing all they knew to deface the landscape. The Professor and I slid down the cliff at the back and found ourselves back in Japan once more. Rough steps took us five or six hundred feet down through dense jungle to the bed of that stream we had followed all the day. The air vibrated with the rush of a hundred torrents, and whenever the eye could pierce the undergrowth it saw a headlong stream breaking itself on a boulder. Up at the hotel we had left the gray chill of a November day and cold that numbed the fingers; down in the gorge we found the climate of Bengal with real steam thrown in. Green bamboo pipes led the hot water

to a score of bathing-houses in whose verandahs Japanese
in blue and white dressing-gowns lounged and smoked.
From unseen thickets came the shouts of those who
bathed, and — oh shame! round the corner strolled a
venerable old lady chastely robed in a white bathing
towel, and not too much of that. Then we went up the
gorge, mopping our brows, and staring to the sky through
arches of rampant foliage.

Japanese maids of fourteen or fifteen are not altogether displeasing to behold. I have not seen more than
twenty or thirty of them. Of these none were in the
least disconcerted at the sight of the stranger. After
all, 'twas but Brighton beach without the bathing-gowns.
At the head of the gorge the heat became greater, and
the hot water more abundant. The joints of the water-
pipes on the ground gave off jets of steam; there was
vapour rising from boulders on the river-bed, and the
stab of a stick into the warm, moist soil was followed by
a little pool of warm water. The existing supply was
not enough for the inhabitants. They were mining for
more in a casual and disconnected fashion. I tried to
crawl down a shaft eighteen inches by two feet in the
hillside, but the steam, which had no effect on the Japanese hide, drove me out. What happens, I wonder,
when the pick strikes the liquid, and the miner has to
run or be parboiled?

In the twilight, when we had reached upper earth
once more and were passing through the one street of
Myanoshita, we saw two small fat cherubs about three
years old taking their evening tub in a barrel sunk under
the eaves of a shop. They feigned great fear, peeping
at us behind outspread fingers, attempting futile dives,

and trying to hide one behind the other in a hundred poses of spankable chubbiness, while their father urged them to splash us. It was the prettiest picture of the day, and one worth coming even to the sticky, paint reeking hotel to see.

*   *   *   *   *   *   *

He was dressed in a black frock-coat, and at first I took him for a missionary as he mooned up and down the empty corridor.

"I have been under a ban for three days," he whispered in a husky voice, "through no fault of mine — no fault of mine. They told me to take the third watch, but they didn't give me a printed notification which I always require, and the manager of this place says that whisky would hurt me. Through no fault of mine, God knows, no fault of mine!"

I do not like being shut up in an echoing wooden hotel next door to a gentleman of the marine persuasion, who is just recovering from D. T., and who talks to himself all through the dark hours.

No. XVIII

"Always speak to the stranger. If he doesn't shoot, the chances are he'll answer you." — *Western Proverb.*

It is a far cry from Myanoshita to Michni and Mandalay. That is why we have met men from both those stations, and have spent a cheerful time talking about dacoits and the Black Mountain Expedition. One of the advantages of foreign travel is that one takes such a keen interest in, and hears so much about, Home. Truly, they change their trains, but not their train of thought, who run across the sea.

"This is a most extraordinary place," said the Professor, red as a boiled lobster. "You sit in your bath and turn on the hot or cold spring, as you choose, and the temperature is phenomenal. Let's go and see where it all comes from, and then let's go away."

There is a place called the Burning Mountain five miles in the hills. There went we, through unbroken loveliness of bamboo-copse, pine wood, grass downs, and pine wood again, while the river growled below. In the end we found an impoverished and second-hand Hell, set out orderly on the side of a raw and bleeding hillside. It looked as though a match-factory had been whelmed

by a landslip. Water, in which bad eggs had been
boiled, stood in blister-lipped pools, and puffs of thin
white smoke went up from the labouring under-earth.
Despite the smell and the sulphur incrustations on the
black rocks, I was disappointed, till I felt the heat of
the ground, which was the heat of a boiler-sheathing.
They call the mountain extinct. If untold tons of
power, cased in a few feet of dirt, be the Japanese
notion of extinction, glad I am that I have not been
introduced to a lively volcano. Indeed, it was not an
overweening notion of my own importance, but a tender
regard for the fire-crust below, and a dread of starting
the machinery by accident, that made me step so deli-
cately, and urge return upon the Professor.

" Huh ! It's only the boiler of your morning bath.
All the sources of the springs are here," said he.

" I don't care. Let 'em alone. Did you never hear
of a boiler bursting ? Don't prod about with your stick
in that amateur way. You'll turn on the tap."

When you have seen a burning mountain you begin to
appreciate Japanese architecture. It is not solid. Every
one is burned out once or twice casually. A business
isn't respectable until it has received its baptism of fire.
But fire is of no importance. The one thing that in-
conveniences a Jap is an earthquake. Consequently, he
arranges his house that it shall fall lightly as a bundle
of broom upon his head. Still further safeguarding
himself, he has no foundations, but the corner-posts rest
on the crowns of round stones sunk in the earth. The
corner-posts take the wave of the shock, and, though the
building may give way like an eel-trap, nothing very
serious happens. This is what epicures of earthquakes

aver. I wait for mine own experiences, but not near a suspected district such as the Burning Mountain.

It was only to escape from one terror to another that I fled Myanoshita. A blue-breeched dwarf thrust me into a dwarf 'rickshaw on spidery wheels, and down the rough road that we had taken four hours to climb ran me clamorously in half an hour. Take all the parapets off the Simla Road and leave it alone for ten years. Then run down the steepest four miles of any section, — not steeper than the drop to the old Gaiety Theatre, — behind one man!

"We couldn't get six hill-men to take us in this style," shouted the Professor as he spun by, his wheels kicking like a duck's foot, and the whole contraption at an angle of thirty. I am proud to think that not even sixty hill-men would have gambolled with a sahib in that disgraceful manner. Nor would any tramway company in the Real East have run its cars to catch a train that used to start last year, but now — rest its soul — is as dead as Queen Anne. This thing a queer little seven-mile tramway accomplished with much dignity. It owned a first-class car and a second-class car, — two horses to each, — and it ran them with a hundred yards headway — the one all but empty, and the other half full. When the very small driver could not control his horses, which happened on the average once every two minutes, he did not waste time by pulling them in. He screwed down the brake and laughed — possibly at the company who had paid for the very elaborate car. Yet he was an artistic driver. He wore no Philistine brass badge. Between the shoulders of his blue jerkin were done in white, three railheads in a circle, and on the skirts as many tram-wheels

conventionalised. Only the Japanese know how to con-
ventionalise a tram-wheel or make a key-pattern of railheads. Though we took twelve hours to cover the thirty
miles that separated us from Yokohama, we admitted
this much while we waited for our train in a village by
the sea. A village of any size is about three miles long
in the main street. Villages with a population of more
than ten thousand souls take rank as towns.

"And yet," said a man at Yokohama that night, "you
have not seen the densest population. That's away in
the western *kens* — districts, as you call them. The folk
really are crowded thereabouts, but virtually poverty
does not exist in the country. You see, an agricultural
labourer can maintain himself and his family, as far
as rice goes, for four cents a day, and the price of fish
is nominal. Rice now costs a hundred pounds to the
dollar. What do you make it by Indian standards?
From twenty to twenty-five seers the rupee. Yes,
that's about it. Well, he gets, perhaps, three dollars
and a-half a month. The people spend a good deal
in pleasuring. They must enjoy themselves. I don't
think they save much. How do they invest their savings? In jewellery? No, not exactly; though you'll
find that the women's hair-pins, which are about the only
jewellery they wear, cost a good deal. Seven and eight
dollars are paid for a good hair-pin, and of course jade
may cost anything. What the women really lock their
money up in is in their *obis* — the things you call sashes.
An *obi* is ten or twelve yards long, and I've known them
sold wholesale for fifty dollars each. Every woman above
the poorest class has at least one good dress of silk and
an *obi*. Yes, all their savings go in dress, and a hand

some dress is always worth having. The western *kens* are the richest taken all round. A skilled mechanic there gets a dollar or dollar and a-half a day, and, as you know, lacquer-workers and inlayers — artists — get two. There's enough money in Japan for all current expenses. They won't borrow any for railroads. They raise it 'emselves. Most progressive people the Japanese are as regards railways. They make them very cheaply, much more cheaply than any European lines. I've some experience, and I take it that two thousand pounds a mile is the average cost of construction. Not on the Tokaido, of course — the line that you came up by. That's a Government line, State built, and a very expensive one. I'm speaking of the Japanese Railway Company with a mileage of three hundred, and the line from Kobé south, and the Kinshin line in the Southern island. There are lots of little companies with a few score miles of line, but all the companies are extending. The reason why the construction is so cheap is the nature of the land. There's no long haulage of rails, because you can nearly always find a creek running far up into the country, and dump out your rails within a few miles of the place where they are wanted. Then, again, all your timber lies to your hand, and your staff are Japs. There are a few European engineers, but they are quite the heads of the departments, and I believe if they were cleared out to-morrow, the Japs would go on building their lines. They know how to make 'em pay. One line started on a State guarantee of eight per cent. It hasn't called for the guarantee yet. It's making twelve per cent on its own hook. There's a very heavy freight traffic in wood and provisions for the big towns, and there's a local traffic that you

can have no idea of unless you've watched it. The people seem to move in twenty-mile circles for business or
pleasure—'specially pleasure. Oh, I tell you, Japan will
be a gridiron of railways before long. In another month
or two you'll be able to travel nearly seven hundred
miles on and by the Tokaido line alone from one end
to the other of the central islands. Getting from east
to west is harder work. The backbone-hills of the country are just cruel, and it will be some time before the
Japs run many lines across. But they'll do it, of course.
Their country must go forward.

"If you want to know anything about their politics,
I'm afraid I can't help you much. They are, so to speak,
drunk with Western liquor, and are sucking it up by the
hogshead. In a few years they will see how much of
what we call civilisation they really want, and how much
they can discard. 'Tisn't as if they had to learn the arts
of life or how to make themselves comfortable. They
knew all that long ago. When their railway system is
completed, and they begin to understand their new Constitution, they will have learned as much as we can teach
'em. That's my opinion; but it needs time to understand this country. I've been a matter of eight or ten
years in it, and my views aren't worth much. I've come
to know some of the old families that used to be of the
feudal nobility. They keep themselves to themselves
and live very quietly. I don't think you'll find many of
them in the official classes. Their one fault is that they
entertain far beyond their means. They won't receive
you informally and take you into their houses. They
raise dancing-girls, or take you to their club and have a
big feed. They don't introduce you to their wives, and

they haven't yet given up the rule of making the wife
eat after the husband. Like the native of India you say?
Well, I am very fond of the Jap; but I suppose he *is* a
native any way you look at him. You wouldn't think
that he is careless in his workmanship and dishonest. A
Chinaman, on an average, is out and away a bigger rogue
than a Jap; but he has sense enough to see that honesty
is the best policy, and to act by that light. A Jap will
be dishonest just to save himself trouble. He's like a
child that way."

How many times have I had to record such an opinion
as the foregoing? Everywhere the foreigner says the
same thing of the neat-handed, polite little people that
live among flowers and babies, and smoke tobacco as
mild as their own manners. I am sorry; but when you
come to think of it, a race without a flaw would be perfect. And then all the other nations of the earth would
rise up and hammer it to pieces. And then there would
be no Japan.

"I'll give you a day to think over things generally,"
said the Professor. "After that we'll go to Nikko and
Tokio. Who has not seen Nikko does not know how to
pronounce the world 'beautiful.'"

Yokohama is not the proper place to arrange impressions in. The Pacific Ocean knocks at your door,
asking to be looked at; the Japanese and American
men-of-war demand serious attention through a tele-
scope; and if you wander about the corridors of the
Grand Hotel, you stop to play with Spanish Generals,
all gold lace and spurs, or are captured by touts for curio-
shops. It is not a nice experience to find a Sahib in a
Panama hat handing you the card of his firm for all the

world like a Delhi silk-merchant. You are inclined to pity that man, until he sits down, gives you a cigar, and tells you all about his diseases, his past career in California, where he was always making money and always losing it, and his hopes for the future. You see then that you are entering upon a new world. Talk to every one you meet, if they show the least dispositon to talk to you, and you will gather, as I have done, a host of stories that will be of use to you hereafter. Unfortunately, they are not all fit for publication. When I tore myself away from the distractions of the outer world, and was just sitting down to write seriously on the Future of Japan, there entered a fascinating man, with heaps of money, who had collected Indian and Japanese curios all his life, and was now come to this country to get some old books which his collection lacked. Can you imagine a more pleasant life than his wanderings over the earth, with untold special knowledge to back each signature of his cheque-book?

In five minutes he had carried me far away from the clattering, fidgetty folk around, to a quiet world where men meditated for three weeks over a bronze, and scoured all Japan for a sword-guard designed by a great artist and — were horribly cheated in the end.

" Who is the best artist in Japan now ? " I asked.

" He died in Tokio, last Friday, poor fellow, and there is no one to take his place. His name was K——, and as a general rule he could never be persuaded to work unless he was drunk. He did his best pictures when he was drunk."

" *Ému*. Artists are never drunk."

" Quite right. I'll show you a sword-guard that he

designed. All the best artists out here do a lot of designing. K—— used to fritter away his time on designs for old friends. Had he stuck to pictures he could have made twice as much. But he never turned out potboilers. When you go to Tokio, make it your business to get two little books of his called *Drunken Sketches* — pictures that he did when he was — *ému.* There is enough dash and go in them to fill half a dozen studios. An English artist studied under him for some time. But K——'s touch was not communicable, though he might have taught his pupil something about technique. Have you ever come across one of K——'s crows? You could tell it anywhere. He could put all the wicked thoughts that ever came into the mind of a crow — and a crow is first cousin to the Devil — on a piece of paper six inches square, with a brush of Indian ink and two turns of his wrist. Look at the sword-guard I spoke of. How is that for feeling? "

On a circular piece of iron four inches in diameter and pierced by the pole for the tang of the blade, poor K——, who died last Friday, had sketched the figure of a coolie trying to fold up a cloth which was bellying to a merry breeze — not a cold wind, but a sportive summer gust. The coolie was enjoying the performance, and so was the cloth. It would all be folded up in another minute and the coolie would go on his way with a grin.

This thing had K—— conceived, and the faithful workman executed, with the lightest touches ot the graver, to the end that it might lie in a collector's cabinet in London.

"Wah! Wah! " I said, and returned it reverently. " It would kill a man who could do that to live after his touch had gone. Well for him he died — but I wish I had seen him. Show me some more."

"I've got a painting by Hokusai — the great artist who lived at the end of the last century and the beginning of this. Even *you* have heard of Hokusai, haven't you?"

"A little. I have heard it was impossible to get a genuine painting with his signature attached."

"That's true; but I've shown this one to the Japanese Government expert in pictures — the man the Mikado consults in cases of doubt — to the first European authority on Japanese art, and of course I have my own opinion to back the signed guarantee of the seller. Look!"

He unrolled a silk-scroll and showed me the figure of a girl in pale blue and grey crêpe, carrying in her arms a bundle of clothes that, as the tub behind her showed, had just been washed. A dark-blue handkerchief was thrown lightly over the left forearm, shoulder, and neck, ready to tie up the clothes when the bundle should be put down. The flesh of the right arm showed through the thin drapery of the sleeve. The right hand merely steadied the bundle from above; the left gripped it firmly from below. Through the stiff blue-black hair showed the outline of the left ear.

That there was enormous elaboration in the picture, from the ornamentation of the hair-pins to the graining of the clogs, did not strike me till after the first five minutes, when I had sufficiently admired the certainty of touch.

"Recollect there is no room for error in painting on silk," said the proud possessor. "The line must stand under any circumstances. All that is possible before

painting is a little dotting with charcoal, which is
rubbed off with a feather-brush.   Did he know anything about drapery or colour or the shape of a
woman?   Is there any one who could teach him more
if he were alive to-day?"

Then we went to Nikk

No. XIX

THE LEGEND OF NIKKO FORD AND THE STORY OF THE
AVOIDANCE OF MISFORTUNE.

A rose-red city, half as old as Time.

FIVE hours in the train took us to the beginning of a
'rickshaw journey of twenty-five miles. The guide un-
earthed an aged cart on Japanese lines, and seduced
us into it by promises of speed and comfort beyond anything that a 'rickshaw could offer. Never go to Nikko
in a cart. The town of departure is full of pack-
ponies who are not used to it, and every third animal
tries to get a kick at his friends in the shafts. This
renders progress sufficiently exciting till the bumpsome-
ness of the road quenches all emotions save one. Nikko
is reached through one avenue of *cryptomerias* — cypress-
like trees eighty feet high, with red or dull silver trunks
and hearse-plume foliage of darkest green. When I say
one avenue, I mean one continuous avenue twenty-five
miles long, the trees so close to each other throughout
that their roots interlace and form a wall of wood on
either side of the sunken road. Where it was necessary
to make a village along the line of march, — that is to
say once every two or three miles, — a few of the giants
had been wrenched out — as teeth are wrenched from a
full-planted jaw — to make room for the houses. Then

the trees closed up as before to mount guard over the road. The banks between which we drove were alight with azaleas, camelias, and violets. "Glorious! Stupendous! Magnificent!" sang the Professor and I in chorus for the first five miles, in the intervals of the bumps. The avenue took not the least notice of our praise except by growing the trees even more closely together. "Vistas of pillared shade" are very pleasant to read about, but on a cold day the ungrateful heart of man could cheerfully dispense with a mile or two of it if that would shorten the journey. We were blind to the beauty around; to the files of pack-ponies with manes like hearth-brooms and the tempers of Eblis kicking about the path; to the pilgrims with blue and white handkerchiefs on their heads, enviable silver-grey leggings on their feet, and Buddha-like babies on their backs; to the trim country drays pulled by miniature cart-horses bringing down copper from the mines and *saki* from the hills; to the colour and movement in the villages where all the little children shouted "Ohio's!" and all the old people laughed. The grey tree-trunks marched us solemnly along over that horrid bad road which had been mended with brushwood, and after five hours we got Nikko in the shape of a long village at the foot of a hill, and capricious Nature, to reward us for our sore bones, laughed on the instant in floods of sunshine. And upon what a mad scene did the light fall! The *cryptomerias* rose in front of us a wall of green darkness, a tearing torrent ran deep-green over blue boulders, and between stream and trees was thrown a blood-red bridge — the sacred bridge of red lacquer that no foot save the Mikado's may press.

Very cunning artists are the Japanese. Long ago a
great-hearted king came to Nikko River and looked across
at the trees, up-stream at the torrent and the hills whence
it came, and down-stream at the softer outlines of the
crops and spurs of wooded mountains. "It needs only
a dash of colour in the foreground to bring this all together," said he, and he put a little child in a blue and
white dressing-gown under the awful trees to judge the
effect. Emboldened by his tenderness, an aged beggar
ventured to ask for alms. Now it was the ancient
privilege of the great to try the temper of their blades
upon beggars and such cattle. Mechanically the king
swept off the old man's head, for he did not wish to be
disturbed. The blood spurted across the granite slabs of
the river-ford in a sheet of purest vermilion. The king
smiled. Chance had solved the problem for him. "Build
a bridge here," he said to the court carpenter, "of just
such a colour as that stuff on the stones. Build also a
bridge of grey stone close by, for I would not forget the
wants of my people." So he gave the little child across
the stream a thousand pieces of gold and went his way.
He had composed a landscape. As for the blood, they
wiped it up and said no more about it; and that is the
story of Nikko Bridge. You will not find it in the
guide-books.

I followed the voice of the river through a rickety
toy-village, across some rough bottom-land, till, crossing
a bridge, I found myself among lichened stones, scrub,
and the blossoms of spring. A hillside, steep and
wooded as the flanks of the red Aravallis, rose on my
left; on my right, the eye travelled from village to crop-
land, crop to towering cypress, and rested at last on the

cold blue of an austere hill-top encircled by streaks of yet unmelted snow. The Nikko hotel stood at the foot of this hill; and the time of the year was May. Then a sparrow came by with a piece of grass in her beak, for she was building her nest; and I knew that the spring was come to Nikko. One is so apt to forget the changes of the year over there with you in India.

Sitting in a solemn line on the banks of the river were fifty or sixty cross-legged images which the untrained eye put down immediately as so many small Buddhas. They had all, even when the lichen had cloaked them with leprosy, the calm port and unwinking regard of the Lord of the World. They are not Buddhas really, but other things — presents from forgotten great men to dead and gone institutions, or else memorials of ancestors. The guide-book will tell you. They were a ghostly crew. As I examined them more closely I saw that each differed from the other. Many of them held in their joined arms a little store of river pebbles, evidently put there by the pious. When I inquired the meaning of the gift from a stranger who passed, he said: "Those so distinguished are images of the God who Plays with Little Children up in the Sky. He tells them stories and builds them houses of pebbles. The stones are put in his arms either that he may not forget to amuse the babies or to prevent his stock running low."

I have no means of telling whether the stranger spoke the truth, but I prefer to believe that tale as gospel truth. Only the Japanese could invent the God who Plays with Little Children. Thereafter the images took a new aspect in my eyes and were no longer "Græco·

Buddhist sculptures," but personal friends. I added a great heap of pebbles to the stock of the cheeriest among them. His bosom was ornamented with small printed slips of prayers which gave him the appearance of a disreputable old parson with his bands in disorder. A little further up the bank of the river was a rough, solitary rock hewn with what men called a Shinto shrine. I knew better: the thing was Hindu, and I looked at the smooth stones on every side for the familiar dab of red paint. On a flat rock overhanging the water were carved certain characters in Sanscrit, remotely resembling those on a Thibetan prayer-wheel. Not comprehending these matters, and grateful that I had brought no guide-book with me, I clambered down to the lip of the river — now compressed into a raging torrent. Do you know the Strid near Bolton — that spot where the full force of the river is pent up in two yards' breadth? The Nikko Strid is an improvement upon the Yorkshire one. The blue rocks are hollowed like soapstone by the rush of the water. They rise above head-level and in spring are tufted with azalea blossom. The stranger of the godlings came up behind me as I basked on a boulder. He pointed up the little gorge of rocks, "Now if I painted that as it stands, every critic in the papers would say I was a liar."

The mad stream came down directly from a blue hill blotched with pink, through a sky-blue gorge also pink-blotched. An obviously impossible pine mounted guard over the water. I would give much to see an accurate representation of that view. The stranger departed growling over some hidden grief — connected with the Academy perhaps.

Hounded on by the Professor, the guide sought me by banks of the river and bade me "come and see temples." Then I fairly and squarely cursed all temples, being stretched at my ease on some warm sand in the hollow of a rock, and ignorant as the grass-shod cattle that tramped the further bank. "Very fine temples," said the guide, "you come and see. By and by temple be shut up because priests make half an hour more time." Nikko time is half an hour ahead of the standard, because the priests of the temples have discovered that travellers arriving at three p.m. try to do all the temples before four — the official hour of closing. This defrauds the church of her dues, so her servants put the clock on, and Nikko, knowing naught of the value of time, is well content.

When I cursed the temples I did a foolish thing, and one for which this poor pen can never make fitting reparation. We went up a hill by way of a flight of grey stone slabs. The *cryptomerias* of the Nikko road were as children to the giants that overshadowed us here. Between their iron-grey boles were flashes of red — the blood-red of the Mikado's bridge. That great king who killed the beggar at the ford had been well pleased with the success of his experiment. Passing under a mighty stone arch we came into a square of splendour alive with the sound of hammers. Thirty or forty men were tapping the pillars and steps of a carnelian shrine heavy with gold. "That," said the guide, impassively, "is a godown. They are renewing the lacquer. First they extract it."

Have you ever "extracted" lacquer from wood? I smote the foot of a pillar with force, and after half a dozen blows chipped off one small fragment of the stuff, in texture like red horn. Betraying no surprise, I demanded the name of a yet more magnificent shrine across the courtyard. It was red lacquered like the others, but above its main door were carved in open work three apes — one with his hands to his ears, another covering his mouth, and a third blinding his eyes.

"That place," said the guide, "used to be a stable when the Daimio kept his horses there. The monkeys are the three who hear no wrong, say no wrong, and see no wrong."

"Of course," I said. "What a splendid device for a stable where the grooms steal the grain!" I was angry because I had grovelled before a godown and a stable, though the round world cannot hold their equals.

We entered a temple, or a tomb, I do not know which, through a gateway of carven pillars. Eleven of them bore a running pattern of trefoil — the apex pointing earthward — the twelfth had its pattern reversed.

"Make 'em all the same — no good," said the guide, emphatically. "Something sure to come bad by an' by. Make one different all right. Save him so. Nothing happen then."

Unless I am mistaken, that voluntarily breaking of the set was the one sacrifice that the designer had made to the great Gods above who are so jealous of the craft of men. For the rest he had done what he pleased — even as a god might have done — with the wood in its gleaming lacquer sheath, with enamel and inlay and carving and bronze, hammered work, and the work of the inspired chisel. When he went to his account he saved himself from the jealousy of his judges, by pointing to the tre

foil pillars for proof that he was only a weak mortal and
in no sense their equals. Men say that never man has
given complete drawings, details, or descriptions of the
temples of Nikko. Only a German would try, and he
would fail in spirit. Only a Frenchman could succeed
in spirit, but he would be inaccurate. I have a recollec-
tion of passing through a door with *cloisonnée* hinges,
with a golden lintel and red lacquer jambs, with panels
of tortoise-shell lacquer and clamps of bronze tracery.
It opened into a half-lighted hall on whose blue ceiling
a hundred golden dragons romped and spat fire. A
priest moved about the gloom with noiseless feet, and
showed me a pot-bellied lantern four feet high, that the
Dutch traders of old time had sent as a present to the
temple. There were posts of red lacquer dusted over
with gold, to support the roof. On one post lay a rib
of lacquer, six inches thick, that had been carved or
punched over with high relief carvings and had set
harder than crystal.

The temple steps were of black lacquer, and the frames
of the sliding screens red. That money, lakhs and lakhs
of money, had been lavished on the wonder impressed
me but little. I wished to know who were the men that,
when the *cryptomerias* were saplings, had sat down and
spent their lives on a niche or corner of the temple, and
dying passed on the duty of adornment to their sons,
though neither father nor child hoped to see the work
completed. This question I asked the guide, who
plunged me in a tangle of Daimios and Shoguns, all
manifestly extracted from a guide-book.

After a while the builder's idea entered into my soul.

He had said: "Let us build blood-red chapels in a

Cathedral." So they planted the Cathedral three hundred years ago, knowing that tree-boles would make the pillars and the sky the roof.

Round each temple stood a small army of priceless bronze or stone lanterns, stamped, as was everything else, with the three leaves that make the Daimio's crest. The lanterns were dark green or lichened grey, and in no way lightened the gloom of the red. Down below, by the sacred bridge, I believed red was a joyous colour. Up the hillside under the trees and the shadow of the temple eaves I saw that it was the hue of sorrow. When the great king killed the beggar at the ford he did not laugh, as I have said. He was very sorry, and said: "Art is Art, and worth any sacrifice. Take that corpse away and pray for the naked soul." Once, in one of the temple courtyards, nature dared to rebel against the scheme of the hillside. Some forest tree, all unimpressed by the *cryptomerias*, had tossed a torrent of tenderest pink flowers down the face of a grey retaining wall that guarded a cutting. It was as if a child had laughed aloud at some magnificence it could not understand.

" You see that cat?" said the guide, pointing out a pot-bellied pussy painted above a door. " That is the Sleeping Cat. The artist he paint it left-handed. We are proud of that cat."

" And did they let him remain left-handed after he had painted that thing?"

" Oh yes. You see he was always left-handed."

The infinite tenderness of the Japanese towards their children extends, it would seem, even to artists. Every guide will take you to see the Sleeping Cat. Don't go. It is bad. Coming down the hill, I learned that all

Nikko was two feet under snow in the winter, and while I was trying to imagine how fierce red, white, and black-green would look under the light of a winter sun I met the Professor murmuring expletives of admiration.

"What have you done? What have you seen?" said he.

"Nothing. I've accumulated a lot of impressions of no use to any one but the owner."

"Which means you are going to slop over for the benefit of the people in India," said the Professor.

And the notion so disgusted me that I left Nikko that very afternoon, the guide clamouring that I had not seen half its glories. "There is a lake," he said; "there are mountains. You must go see!"

"I will return to Tokio and study the modern side of Japan. This place annoys me because I do not understand it."

"Yet I am *the* good guide of Yokohama," said the guide.

No. XX

"And the Duke said, 'Let there be cavalry,' and there were cavalry. And he said, 'Let them be slow,' and they were slow, d—d slow; and the Japanese Imperial Horse called he them."

I WAS wrong. I know it. I ought to have clamoured at the doors of the Legation for a pass to see the Imperial Palace. I ought to have investigated Tokio and called upon some of the political leaders of the Liberal and Radical parties. There are a hundred things which I ought to have done, but somehow or other the bugles began to blare through the chill of the morning, and I heard the tramp of armed men under my window. The parade-ground was within a stone's throw of the Tokio hotel; the Imperial troops were going on parade. Would *you* have bothered your head about politics or temples? I ran after them.

It is rather difficult to get accurate information about the Japanese army. It seems to be in perpetual throes of reorganisation. At present, so far as one can gather, it is about one hundred and seventy thousand strong. Everybody has to serve for three years, but payment of one hundred dollars will shorten the term of service by one year at least. This is what a man who had gone through the mill told me. He capped his information

with this verdict: "English army no use. Only navy
any good. Have seen two hundred English army. No
use."

On the parade-ground they had a company of foot
and a wing of what, for the sake of brevity, I will call
cavalry under instruction. The former were being put
through some simple evolutions in close order; the latter
were variously and singularly employed. To the former
I took off the hat of respect; at the latter I am ashamed
to say I pointed the finger of derision. But let me try
to describe what I saw. The likeness of the Jap infantryman to the Gurkha grows when you see him in bulk.
Thanks to their wholesale system of conscription the
quality of conscripts varies immensely. I have seen
scores of persons with spectacles whom it were base flattery to call soldiers, and who I hope were in the medical
or commissariat departments. Again I have seen dozens
of bull-necked, deep-chested, flat-backed, thin-flanked
little men who were as good as a colonel commanding
could desire. There was a man of the 2d Infantry whom
I met at an up-country railway station. He carried just
the proper amount of insolent swagger that a soldier
should, refused to answer any questions of mine, and
parted the crowd round him without ceremony. A
Gurkha of the Prince of Wales' Own could not have
been trimmer. In the crush of a ticket-collecting — we
both got out together — I managed to run my hand over
that small man's forearm and chest. They must have
a very complete system of gymnastics in the Japanese
army, and I would have given much to have stripped my
friend and seen how he peeled. If the 2d Infantry are
equal to sample, they are good.

The men on parade at Tokio belonged either to the
4th or the 9th, and turned out with their cowskin
valises strapped, but I think not packed. Under full
kit, such as I saw on the sentry at Osaka Castle, they
ought to be much too heavily burdened. Their officers
were as miserable a set of men as Japan could furnish —
spectacled, undersized even for Japan, hollow-backed and
hump-shouldered. They squeaked their words of command and had to trot by the side of their men to keep
up with them. The Jap soldier has the long stride of
the Gurkha, and he doubles with the easy lope of the
'rickshaw coolie. Throughout the three hours that I
watched them they never changed formation but once,
when they doubled in pairs across the plain, their rifles
at the carry. Their step and intervals were as good as
those of our native regiments, but they wheeled rather
promiscuously, and were not checked for this by their
officers. So far as my limited experience goes, their formation was not Ours, but continental. The words of
command were as beautifully unintelligible as anything
our parade-grounds produce; and between them the
officers of each half-company vehemently harangued
their men, and shook their swords at 'em in distinctly
unmilitary style. The precision of their movements
was beyond praise. They enjoyed three hours of steady
drill, and in the rare intervals when they stood easy to
draw breath I looked for slackness all down the ranks,
inasmuch as "standing easy" is the crucial test of men
after the first smartness of the morning has worn off.
They stood "easy," neither more nor less, but never a
hand went to a shoe or stock or button while they were
so standing. When they knelt, still in this queer column

of company, I understood the mystery of the long-sword
bayonet which has puzzled me sorely. I had expected
to see the little fellows lifted into the air as the bayonet-
sheath took ground; but they were not. They kicked it
sideways as they dropped. All the same, the authorities
tie men to the bayonets instead of bayonets to the men.
When at the double there was no grabbing at the car-
tridge pouch with one hand or steadying the bayonet
with the other, as may be seen any day at running-firing
on Indian ranges. They ran cleanly — as our Gurkhas
run.

It was an unchristian thought, but I would have given
a good deal to see that company being blooded on an
equal number of Our native infantry — just to know how
they would work. If they have pluck, and there is not
much in their past record to show that they have not,
they ought to be first-class enemies. Under British
officers instead of the little anatomies at present provided, and with a better rifle, they should be as good as
any troops recruited east of Suez. I speak here only
for the handy little men I saw. The worst of conscription is that it sweeps in such a mass of fourth and fifth-
rate citizens who, though they may carry a gun, are
likely, by their own excusable ineptitude, to do harm
to the morale and set-up of a regiment. In their walks
abroad the soldiery never dream of keeping step. They
tie things to their side-arms, they carry bundles, they
slouch, and dirty their uniforms.

And so much for a raw opinion on Japanese infantry.
The cavalry were having a picnic on the other side of the
parade-ground — circling right and left by sections, trying
to do something with a troop, and so forth. I would fain

believe that the gentlemen I saw were recruits. But they
wore all their arms, and their officers were just as clever
as themselves. Half of them were in white fatigue-dress
and flat cap, — and wore half-boots of brown leather
with short hunting-spurs and black straps; no chains.
They carried carbine and sword — the sword fixed to
the man, and the carbine slung over the back. No mar-
tingales, but breastplates and crupper, a huge, heavy
saddle, with single hide-girth, over two *numdahs*, completed the equipment which a thirteen-hand pony, all
mane and tail, was trying to get rid of. When you
thrust a two-pound bit and bridoon into a small pony's
mouth, you hurt his feelings. When the riders wear,
as did my friends, white worsted gloves, they cannot
take a proper hold of the reins. When they ride with
both hands, sitting well on the mount's neck, knuckles
level with its ears and the stirrup leathers as short as
they can be, the chances of the pony getting rid of the
rider are manifestly increased. Never have I seen such
a wild dream of equitation as the Tokio parade-ground
showed. Do you remember the picture in *Alice in Wonderland*, just before Alice found the Lion and the Uni-
corn; when she met the armed men coming through the
woods? I thought of that, and I thought of the White
Knight in the same classic, and I laughed aloud. Here
were a set of very fair ponies, sure-footed as goats,
mostly entires, and full of go. Under Japanese weights
they would have made very thorough mounted infantry.
And here was this blindly imitative nation trying to
turn them into heavy cavalry. As long as the little
beasts were gravely trotting in circles they did not mind
their work. But when it came to slashing at the Turk's

head they objected very much indeed. I affiliated myself to a section who, armed with long wooden swords, were enjoying some Turk's-heading. Out started a pony at the gentlest of canters, while the rider bundled all the reins into one hand, and held his sword like a lance. Then the pony shied a little shy, shook his shaggy head, and began to passage round the Turk's head. There was no pressure of knee or rein to tell him what was wanted. The man on top began kicking with the spurs from shoulder to rump, and shaking up the ironmongery in the poor brute's mouth. The pony could neither rear, nor kick, nor buck; but it shook itself free of the incubus who slid off. Three times I saw this happen. The catastrophe didn't rise to the dignity of a fall. It was the blundering collapse of incompetence plus worsted gloves, two-handed riding, and a haystack of equipment. Very often the pony went at the post, and the man delivered a back-handed cut at the Turk's head which nearly brought him out of his world-too-wide saddle. Again and again this solemn performance was repeated. I can honestly say that the ponies are very willing to break rank and leave their companions, which is what an English troop-horse fails in; but I fancy this is more due to the urgent private affairs of the pony than any skill in training. The troops charged once or twice in a terrifying canter. When the men wished to stop they leaned back and tugged, and the pony put his head to the ground, and bored all he knew. They charged me, but I was merciful, and forebore to empty half the saddles, as I assuredly could have done by throwing up my arms and yelling "Hi!" The saddest thing of all was the painful conscientiousness displayed by all the

2 **

performers in the circus. They had to turn these rats into cavalry. They knew nothing about riding, and what they did know was wrong; but the rats must be made troop-horses. Why wouldn't the scheme work? There was a patient, pathetic wonder on the faces of the men that made me long to take one of them in my arms and try to explain things to him — bridles, for instance, and the futility of hanging on by the spurs. Just when the parade was over, and the troops were ambling off, Providence sent diagonally across the parade-ground, at a gallop, a big, rawboned man on a lathy-red American horse. The brute cracked his nostrils, and switched his flag abroad, and romped across the plain, while his rider dropped one hand and sat still, swaying lightly from the hips. The two served to scale the surroundings. Some one really ought to tell the Mikado that ponies were never intended for dragoons.

If the changes and chances of military service ever send you against Japanese troops, be tender with their cavalry. They mean no harm. Put some fusees down for the horses to step on, and send a fatigue-party out to pick up the remnants. But if you meet Japanese infantry, led by a Continental officer, commence firing early and often and at the longest ranges compatible with getting at them. They are bad little men who know too much.

Having thoroughly settled the military side of the nation exactly as my Japanese friend at the beginning of this letter settled Us, — on the strength of two hundred men caught at random, — I devoted myself to a consideration of Tokio. I am wearied of temples. Their monotony of splendour makes my head ache. You also will weary of temples unless you are an artist, and then you will be disgusted with yourself. Some folk say that Tokio covers an area equal to London. Some folk say that it is not more than ten miles long and eight miles broad. There are a good many ways of solving the question. I found a tea-garden situated on a green plateau far up a flight of steps, with pretty girls smiling on every step. From this elevation I looked forth over the city, and it stretched away from the sea, as far as the eye could reach — one grey expanse of packed house-roof, the perspective marked by numberless factory chimneys. Then I went several miles away and found a park, another eminence, and some more tea-girls prettier than the last; and, looking again, the city stretched out in a new direction as far as the eye could reach. Taking the scope of the eye on a clear day at eighteen miles, I make Tokio thirty-six miles long by thirty-six miles broad exactly; and there may be some more which I missed. The place roared with life through all its quarters. Double lines of trams ran down the main streets for mile on mile, rows of omnibuses stood at the principal railway station, and the "Compagnie General des Omnibus de Tokio" paraded the streets with gold and vermilion cars. All the trams were full, all the private and public omnibuses were full, and the streets were full of 'rickshaws. From the sea-shore to the shady green park, from the park to the dim distance, the land pullulated with people.

Here you saw how Western civilisation had eaten into them. Every tenth man was attired in Europe clothes from hat to boots. It is a queer race. It can parody every type of humanity to be met in a large

English town. Fat and prosperous merchant with mutton-chop whiskers; mild-eyed, long-haired professor of science, his clothes baggy about him; schoolboy in Eton jacket, broadcloth trousers; young clerk, member of the Clapham Athletic Club in tennis flannels; artisans in sorely worn tweeds; top-hatted lawyer with clean-shaven upper lip and black leather bag; sailor out of work; and counter-jumper; all these and many, many more you shall find in the streets of Tokio in half an hour's walk. But when you come to speak to the imitation, behold it can only talk Japanese. You touch it, and it is not what you thought. I fluctuated down the streets addressing myself to the most English-looking folk I saw. They were polite with a graciousness that in no way accorded with their raiment, but they knew not a word of my tongue. One small boy in the uniform of the Naval College said suddenly: "I spik Inglees," and collapsed. The rest of the people in our clothes poured their own vernacular upon my head. Yet the shop-signs were English, the tramway under my feet was English gauge, the commodities sold were English, and the notices on the streets were in English. It was like walking in a dream. I reflected. Far away from Tokio and off the line of rail I had met men like these men in the streets. Perfectly dressed Englishmen to the outer eye, but dumb. The country must be full of their likes.

"Good gracious! Here is Japan going to run its own civilisation without learning a language in which you can say Damn satisfactorily. I must inquire into this."

Chance had brought me opposite the office of a newspaper, and I ran in demanding an editor. He came —

the Editor of the *Tokio Public Opinion*, a young man in a black frock-coat. There are not many editors in other parts of the world who would offer you tea and a cigarette ere beginning a conversation. My friend had but little English. His paper, though the name was printed in English, was Japanese. But he knew his business. Almost before I had explained my errand, which was the pursuit of miscellaneous information, he began: " You are English. How you think now the American Revision Treaty? " Out came a note-book and I sweated cold. It was not in the bargain that he should interview me.

"There's a great deal," I answered, remembering Sir Roger, of blessed memory, — "a great deal to be said on both sides. The American Revision Treaty — h'm — demands an enormous amount of matured consideration and may safely be referred — "

"But we of Japan are now civilised."

Japan says that she is now civilised. That is the crux of the whole matter so far as I understand it. " Let us have done with the idiotic system of treaty-ports and passports for the foreigner who steps beyond them," says Japan in effect. " Give us our place among the civilised nations of the earth, come among us, trade with us, hold land in our midst. Only be subject to our jurisdiction and submit to our — tariffs." Now since one or two of the foreign nations have won special tariffs for their goods in the usual way, they are not over-anxious to become just ordinary folk. The effect of accepting Japan's views would be excellent for the individual who wanted to go up-country and make his money, but bad for the nation. For Our nation in particular.

All the same I was not prepared to have my ignorance of a burning question put down in any note-book save my own. I Gladstoned about the matter with the longest words I could. My friend recorded them much after the manner of Count Smorltork. Then I attacked him on the subject of civilisation — speaking very slowly because he had a knack of running two words of mine together, and turning them into something new.

"You are right," said he. "We are becoming civilised. But not too quick, for that is bad. Now there are two parties in the State — the Liberal and the Radical: one Count he lead one, one Count lead the other. The Radical say that we should swiftly become all English. The Liberal he says not so quick, because that nation which too swiftly adopt other people's customs he decay. That question of civilisation and the American Revision Treaty he occupied our chief attentions. Now we are not so zealous to become civilised as we were two — three years gone. Not so quick — that is our watchword. Yes."

If matured deliberation be the wholesale adoption of imperfectly understood arrangements, I should dearly like to see Japan in a hurry. We discussed comparative civilisations for a short time, and I protested feebly against the defilement of the streets of Tokio by rows of houses built after glaring European models. Surely there is no need to discard your own architecture, I said.

"Ha," snorted the chief of the *Public Opinion*. "You call it picturesque. I call it too. Wait till he light up — incendiate. A Japanese house then is one only fire box. *That* is why we think good to build in European fashion. I tell you, and you must believe, that we take up no change without thinking upon it. Truth, indeed, it is not because we are curious children, wanting new things, as some people have said. We have done with that season of picking up things and throwing them down again. You see?"

"Where did you pick up your Constitution, then?"

I did not know what the question would bring forth, yet I ought to have been wise. The first question that a Japanese on the railway asks an Englishman is: "Have you got the English translation of our Constitution?" All the book-stalls sell it in English and Japanese, and all the papers discuss it. The child is not yet three months old.

"Our Constitution?—That was promised to us—promised twenty years ago. Fourteen years ago the provinces they have been allowed to elect their big men—their heads. Three years ago they have been allowed to have assemblies, and thus Civil Liberty was assured."

I was baffled here for some time. In the end I thought I made out that the municipalities had been given certain control over police funds and the appointment of district officials. I may have been entirely wrong, but the editor bore me along on a torrent of words, his body rocking and his arms waving with the double agony of twisting a foreign tongue to his service and explaining the to-be-taken-seriouslyness of Japan. Whack come the little hand on the little table, and the little tea-cups jumped again.

"Truly, and indeed, this Constitution of ours has *not* come too soon. It proceeded step-by. You understand that? Now your Constitution, the Constitutions of the

foreign nations, are all bloody — bloody Constitutions.
Ours has come step-by. We did not fight as the barons
fought with King John at Runnymede."

This was a quotation from a speech delivered at Otsu.
a few days previously, by a member of the Government.
I grinned at the brotherhood of editors all the world
over. Up went the hand anew.

"We shall be happy with this Constitution and a
people civilised among civilisations."

"Of course. But what will you actually do with it?
A Constitution is rather a monotonous thing to work
after the fun of sending members to Parliament has died
out. You have a Parliament, have you not?"

"Oh yes, *with* parties — Liberal and Radical."

"Then they will both tell lies to you and to each
other. Then they will pass bills, and spend their time
fighting each other. Then all the foreign governments
will discover that you have no fixed policy."

"Ah, yes. But the Constitution." The little hands
were crossed in his lap. The cigarette hung limply
from his mouth.

"No fixed policy. Then, when you have sufficiently
disgusted the foreign Powers, they will wait until the
Liberals and Radicals are fighting very hard, and then
they will blow you out of the water."

"You are not making fun? I do not quite understand," said he. "Your Constitutions are all so bloody."

"Yes. That is exactly what they are. You are very
much in earnest about yours, are you not?"

"Oh yes, we all talk politics now."

"And write politics, of course. By the way, under what
—h'm. arrangements with the Government is a Japanese

paper published? I mean, must you pay anything before starting a press?"

"Literary, scientific, and religious papers — no. Quite free. All purely political papers pay five hundred yen — give to the Government to keep, or else some man says he will pay."

"You must give security, you mean?"

"I do not know, but sometimes the Government can keep the money. We are purely political."

Then he asked questions about India, and appeared astonished to find that the natives there possessed considerable political power, and controlled districts.

"But have you a Constitution in India?"

"I am afraid that we have not."

"Ah!"

He crushed me there, and I left very humbly, but cheered by the promise that the *Tokio Public Opinion* would contain an account of my words. Mercifully, that respectable journal is printed in Japanese, so the hash will not be served up to a large table. I would give a good deal to discover what meaning he attached to my forecast of Constitutional government in Japan.

"We all talk politics now." That was the sentence which remained to me. It was true talk. Men of the Educational Department in Tokio told me that the students would "talk politics" by the hour if you allowed them. At present they were talking in the abstract about their new plaything, the Constitution, with its Upper House and its Lower House, its committees, its questions of supply, its rules of procedure, and all the other skittles we have played with for six hundred years.

Japan is the second Oriental country which has made

it impossible for a strong man to govern alone. This she has done of her own free will. India, on the other hand, has been forcibly ravished by the Secretary of State and the English M. P.

Japan is luckier than India.

Very sadly did we leave it, but we gave our hearts in pledge
To the pine above the city, to the blossoms by the hedge,
To the cherry and the maple and the plum tree and the peach,
And the babies — Oh, the babies ! — romping fatly under each.
Eastward ho ! Across the water see the black bow drives and
     swings
From the land of Little Children, where the Babies are the Kings.

THE Professor discovered me in meditation amid tea-
girls at the back of the Ueno Park in the heart of Tokio.
My 'rickshaw coolie sat by my side drinking tea from
daintiest china, and eating maccaroons. I thought of
Sterne's donkey and smiled vacuously into the blue
above the trees. The tea-girls giggled. One of them
captured my spectacles, perched them on her own
snubby-chubby nose, and ran about among her cackling
fellows.

"And loose thy fingers in the tresses of The cypress-
slender minister of wine," quoted the Professor, coming
round a booth suddenly. "Why aren't you at the
Mikado's garden party ? "

"Because he didn't invite me, and, anyhow, he wears

Europe clothes — so does the Empress — so do all the Court people. Let's sit down and consider things. This people puzzles me."

And I told my story of the interview with the Editor of the *Tokio Public Opinion*. The Professor had been making investigation into the Educational Department. "And further," said he at the end of the tale, "the ambition of the educated student is to get a place under Government. Therefore he comes to Tokio: will accept any situation at Tokio that he may be near to his chance."

"Whose son is that student?"

"Son of the peasant, yeoman farmer, and shopkeeper, *ryot*, *tehsildar*, and *bunnia*. While he waits he imbibes Republican leanings on account of the nearness of Japan to America. He talks and writes and debates, and is convinced he can manage the Empire better than the Mikado."

"Does he go away and start newspapers to prove that?"

"He may; but it seems to be unwholesome work. A paper can be suspended without reason given under the present laws; and I'm told that one enterprising editor has just got three years' simple imprisonment for caricaturing the Mikado."

"Then there is yet hope for Japan. I can't quite understand how a people with a taste for fighting and quick artistic perceptions can care for the things that delight our friends in Bengal."

"You make the mistake of looking on the Bengali as unique. So he is in his own peculiar style; but I take it that the drunkenness of Western wine affects all

Oriental folk in much the same way. What misleads you is that very likeness. Followest thou? Because a Jap struggles with problems beyond his grip in much the same phraseology as a Calcutta University student, and discusses Administration with a capital A, you lump Jap and Chatterjee together."

"No, I don't. Chatterjee doesn't sink his money in railway companies, or sit down and provide for the proper sanitation of his own city, or of his own notion cultivate the graces of life, as the Jap does. He is like the *Tokio Public Opinion* — 'purely political.' He has no art whatever, he has no weapons, and there is no power of manual labour in him. Yet he is like the Jap in the pathos of his politics. Have you ever studied Pathetic Politics? *Why* is he like the Jap?"

"Both drunk, I suppose," said the Professor. "Get that girl to give back your gig-lamps, and you will be able to see more clearly into the soul of the Far East."

"The 'Far East' hasn't got a soul. She swapped it for a Constitution on the Eleventh of February last. Can any Constitution make up for the wearing of Europe clothes? I saw a Jap lady just now in full afternoon calling-kit. She looked atrocious. Have you seen the later Japanese art — the pictures on the fans and in the shop windows? They are faithful reproductions of the changed life — telegraph poles down the streets, conventionalised tram-lines, top-hats, and carpet-bags in the hands of the men. The artists can make those things almost passable, but when it comes to conventionalising a Europe dress, the effect is horrible."

"Japan wishes to take her place among civilised nations," said the Professor.

"That's where the pathos comes in. It's enough to make you weep to watch this misdirected effort — this wallowing in unloveliness for the sake of recognition at the hands of men who paint their ceilings white, their grates black, their mantelpieces French grey, and their carriages yellow and red. The Mikado wears blue and gold and red, his guards wear orange breeches with a stone-blue stripe down them; the American missionary teaches the Japanese girl to wear bangs — "shingled bangs" — on her forehead, plait her hair into a pigtail, and to tie it up with magenta and cobalt ribbons. The German sells them the offensive chromos of his own country and the labels of his beer-bottles. Allen and Ginter devastate Tokio with their blood-red and grass-green tobacco-tins. And in the face of all these things the country wishes to progress toward civilisation! I have read the entire Constitution of Japan, and it is dearly bought at the price of one of the kaleidoscope omnibuses plying in the street there."

"Are you going to inflict all that nonsense on them at home?" said the Professor.

"I am. For this reason. In the years to come, when Japan has sold her birthright for the privilege of being cheated on equal terms by her neighbours; when she has so heavily run into debt for her railways and public works that the financial assistance of England and annexation is her only help; when the Daimios through poverty have sold the treasures of their houses to the curio-dealer, and the dealer has sold them to the English collector; when all the people wear slop-trousers and ready-made petticoats, and the Americans have established soap factories on the rivers and a boarding-house on the top of Fujiyama, some one will turn up the files of the *Pioneer* and say: 'This thing was prophesied.' Then they will be sorry that they began tampering with the great sausage-machine of civilisation. What is put into the receiver must come out at the spout; but it must come out mincemeat. *Dixi!* And now let us go to the tomb of the Forty-Seven Ronins."

"It has been said some time ago, and much better than you can say it," said the Professor, *apropos* of nothing that I could see.

Distances are calculated by the hour in Tokio. Forty minutes in a 'rickshaw, running at full speed, will take you a little way into the city; two hours from the Ueno Park brings you to the tomb of the famous Forty-Seven, passing on the way the very splendid temples of Shiba, which are all fully described in the guide-books. Lacquer, gold-inlaid bronze-work, and crystals carved with the words "Om" and "Shri" are fine things to behold, but they do not admit of very varied treatment in print. In one tomb of one of the temples was a room of lacquer panels overlaid with gold leaf. An animal of the name of V. Gay had seen fit to scratch his entirely uninteresting name on the gold. Posterity will take note that V. Gay never cut his fingernails, and ought not to have been trusted with anything prettier than a hog-trough.

"It is the handwriting upon the wall," I said.

"Presently there will be neither gold nor lacquer — nothing but the finger-marks of foreigners. Let us pray for the soul of V. Gay all the same. Perhaps he was a missionary."

*   *   *   *   *   *   *

The Japanese papers occasionally contain, sandwiched between notes of railway, mining, and tram concessions, announcements like the following: " Dr. —— committed *hara-kiri* last night at his private residence in such and such a street. Family complications are assigned as the reason of the act." Nor does *hara-kiri* merely mean suicide by any method. *Hara-kiri* is *hara-kiri*, and the private performance is even more ghastly than the official one. It is curious to think that any one of the dapper little men with top-hats and reticules who have a Constitution of their own, may in time of mental stress, strip to the waist, shake their hair over their brows, and, after prayer, rip themselves open. When you come to Japan, look at Farsari's *hara-kiri* pictures and his photos of the last crucifixion (twenty years ago) in Japan. Then at Deakin's, inquire for the modelled head of a gentleman who was not long ago executed in Tokio. There is a grim fidelity in the latter work of art that will make you uncomfortable. The Japanese, in common with the rest of the East, have a strain of blood-thirstiness in their compositions. It is very carefully veiled now, but some of Hokusai's pictures show it, and show that not long ago the people revelled in its outward expression. Yet they are tender to all children beyond the tenderness of the West, courteous to each other beyond the courtesy of the English, and polite to the foreigner alike in the big towns and in the Mofussil. What they will be after their Constitution has been working for three generations the Providence that made them what they are alone knows!

All the world seems ready to proffer them advice. Colonel Olcott is wandering up and down the country

now, telling them that the Buddhist religion needs refor-
mation, offering to reform it, and eating with ostentation
rice gruel which is served to him in cups by admiring
handmaidens. A wanderer from Kioto tells me that in
the Chion-in, loveliest of all the temples, he saw only
three days ago the Colonel mixed up with a procession
of Buddhist priests, just such a procession as the one I
tried vainly to describe, and "tramping about as if the
whole show belonged to him." You cannot appreciate
the solemnity of this until you have seen the Colonel and
the Chion-in temple. The two are built on entirely
different lines, and they don't seem to harmonise. It
only needs now Madame Blavatsky, cigarette in mouth,
under the *cryptomerias* of Nikko, and the return of Mr.
Caine, M. P., to preach the sin of drinking *saki*, and the
menagerie would be full.

Something should be done to America. There are
many American missionaries in Japan, and some of
them construct clapboard churches and chapels for
whose ugliness no creed could compensate. They further instil into the Japanese mind wicked ideas of "Progress," and teach that it is well to go ahead of your
neighbour, to improve your situation, and generally to
thresh yourself to pieces in the battle of existence.
They do not mean to do this; but their own restless
energy enforces the lesson. The American is objectiona-
ble. And yet — this is written from Yokohama — how
pleasant in every way is a nice American whose tongue
is cleansed of "right there," "all the time," "noos,"
"revoo," "raound," and the Falling Cadence. I have
met such an one even now — a Californian ripened in
Spain, matured in England, polished in Paris, and yes

2ʙ

always a Californian. His voice and manners were soft alike, temperate were his judgments and temperately expressed, wide was his range of experience, genuine his humour, and fresh from the mint of his mind his reflections. It was only at the end of the conversation that he startled me a little.

"I understand that you are going to stay some time in California. Do you mind my giving you a little advice? I am speaking now of towns that are still rather brusque in their manners. When a man offers you a drink accept at once, and then stand drinks all round. I don't say that the second part of the programme is as necessary as the first, but it puts you on a perfectly safe footing. Above all, remember that where you are going you must never carry anything. The men you move among will do that for you. They have been accustomed to it. It is in some places, unluckily, a matter of life and death as well as daily practice to draw first. I have known really lamentable accidents occur from a man carrying a revolver when he did not know what to do with it. Do you understand anything about revolvers?"

"N—no," I stammered, "of course not."

"Do you think of carrying one?"

"Of course not. I don't want to kill myself."

"Then you are safe. But remember you will be moving among men who go heeled, and you will hear a good deal of talk about the thing and a great many tall stories. You may listen to the yarns, but you must not conform to the custom however much you may feel tempted. You invite your own death if you lay your hand on a weapon you don't understand. No man flourishes a revolver in a bad place. It is produced for one specified purpose and produced before you can wink."

"But surely if you draw first you have an advantage over the other man," said I, valorously.

"You think so? Let me show you. I have no use for any weapon, but I believe I have one about me somewhere. An ounce of demonstration is worth a ton of theory. Your pipe-case is on the table. My hands are on the table too. Use that pipe case as a revolver and as quickly as you can."

I used it in the approved style of the penny dreadful — pointed it with a stiff arm at my friend's head. Before I knew how it came about the pipe case had quitted my hand, which was caught close to the funny-bone and tingled horribly. I heard four persuasive clicks under the table almost before I knew that my arm was useless. The gentleman from California had jerked out his pistol from its pocket and drawn the trigger four times, his hand resting on his hip while I was lifting my right arm.

"Now, do you believe?" he said. "Only an Englishman or an Eastern man fires from the shoulder in that melodramatic manner. I had you safe before your arm went out, merely because I happened to know the trick; and there are men out yonder who in a trouble could hold me as safe as I held you. They don't reach round for their revolver, as novelists say. It's here in front, close to the second right brace-button, and it is fired, without aim, at the other man's stomach. You will understand now why in event of a dispute you should show very clearly that you are unarmed. You needn't hold up your hands ostentatiously; keep them out of your pockets, or somewhere where your friend can see them. No man will touch you then. Or if he does, he is pretty sure to be shot by the general sense of the room."

"That must be a singular consolation to the corpse," I said.

"I see I've misled you. Don't fancy that any part in America is as free and easy as my lecture shows. Only in a few really tough towns do you require *not* to own a revolver. Elsewhere you are all right. Most Americans of my acquaintance have got into the habit of carrying something; but it's only a habit. They'd never dream of using it unless they are hard pressed. It's the man who draws to enforce a proposition about canning peaches, orange-culture, or town lots or water-rights that's a nuisance."

"Thank you," I said faintly. "I purpose to investigate these things later on. I'm much obliged to you for your advice."

When he had departed it struck me that, in the language of the East, "he might have been pulling my leg." But there remained no doubt whatever as to his skill with the weapon he excused so tenderly.

I put the case before the Professor. "We will go to America before you forejudge it altogether," said he. "To America in an American ship will we go, and say good-by to Japan." That night we counted the gain of our sojourn in the Land of Little Children more closely than many men count their silver. Nagasaki with the grey temples, green hills, and all the wonder of a first-seen shore; the Inland Sea, a thirty-hour panorama of passing islets drawn in grey and buff and silver for our delight; Kobé, where we fed well and went to a theatre; Osaka of the canals and the peach blossom; Kioto — happy, lazy, sumptuous Kioto, and the blue rapids and innocent delights of Arashima; Otzu on the shoreless, rainy lake; Myanoshita in the hills; Kamakura by the tumbling Pacific, where the great god Buddha sits and equably hears the centuries and the seas murmur in his ears; Nikko, fairest of all places under the sun; Tokio, the two-thirds civilised and altogether progressive warren of humanity; and composite Franco-American Yokohama; we renewed them all, sorting out and putting aside our special treasures of memory. If we stayed longer, we might be disillusioned, and yet—surely, that would be impossible.

"What sort of mental impression do you carry away?" said the Professor.

"A tea-girl in fawn-coloured crêpe under a cherry tree all blossom. Behind her, green pines, two babies, and a hog-backed bridge spanning a bottle-green river running over blue boulders. In the foreground a little policeman in badly fitting Europe clothes drinking tea from blue and white china on a black lacquered stand. Fleecy white clouds above and a cold wind up the street," I said, summarising hastily.

"Mine is a little different. A Japanese boy in a flatheaded German cap and baggy Eton jacket; a King taken out of a toy-shop, a railway taken out of a toyshop, hundreds of little Noah's Ark trees and fields made of green-painted wood. The whole neatly packed in a camphor-wood box with an explanatory book called the Constitution—price twenty cents."

"You looked on the darker side of things. But what's the good of writing impressions? Every man has to get his own at first hand. Suppose I give an itinerary of what we saw?"

"You couldn't do it," said the Professor, blandly.

"Besides, by the time the next Anglo-Indian comes this way there will be a hundred more miles of railway and all the local arrangements will have changed. Write that a man should come to Japan without any plans. The guide-books will tell him a little, and the men he meets will tell him ten times more. Let him get first a good guide at Kobé, and the rest will come easily enough. An itinerary is only a fresh manifestation of that unbridled egoism which—"

"I shall write that a man can do himself well from Calcutta to Yokohama, stopping at Rangoon, Moulmein, Penang, Singapur, Hong-Kong, Canton, and taking a month in Japan, for about sixty pounds—rather less than more. But if he begins to buy curios, that man is lost. Five hundred rupees cover his month in Japan and allow him every luxury. Above all, he should bring with him thousands of cheroots—enough to serve him till he reaches 'Frisco. Singapur is the last place on the line where you can buy Burmas. Beyond that point wicked men sell Manila cigars with fancy names for ten, and Havanas for thirty-five, cents. No one inspects your boxes till you reach 'Frisco. Bring, therefore, at least one thousand cheroots."

"Do you know, it seems to me you have a very queer sense of proportion?"

And that was the last word the Professor spoke on Japanese soil.

No. XXII

> " Then spoke der Captain Stossenheim
> Who had theories of God,
> 'Oh, Breitmann, this is judgment on
> Der ways dot you have trod.
> You only lifs to enjoy yourself
> While you yourself agree
> Dot self-development requires
> Der religious Idee.'" — *C. G. Leland.*

THIS is America. They call her the *City of Peking*, and she belongs to the Pacific Mail Company, but for all practical purposes she is the United States. We are divided between missionaries and generals — generals who were at Vicksburg and Shiloh, and German by birth, but more American than the Americans, who in confidence tell you that they are not generals at all, but only brevet majors of militia corps. The missionaries are perhaps the queerest portion of the cargo. Did you ever hear an English minister lecture for half an hour on the freight-traffic receipts and general working of, let us say, the Midland? The Professor has been sitting at the feet of a keen-eyed, close-bearded, swarthy man who expounded unto him kindred mysteries with a fluency and precision that a city leader-writer might have envied. "Who's your

financial friend with the figures at his fingers' ends?"
I asked. "Missionary — Presbyterian Mission to the
Japs," said the Professor. I laid my hand upon my
mouth and was dumb.

As a counterpoise to the missionaries, we carry men
from Manila — lean Scotchmen who gamble once a
month in the Manila State lottery and occasionally
turn up trumps. One, at least, drew a ten-thousand-
dollar prize last December and is away to make merry
in the New World. Everybody on the staff of an
American steamer this side the Continent seems to
gamble steadily in that lottery, and the talk of the
smoking-room runs almost entirely on prizes won by
accident or lost through a moment's delay. The tickets
are sold more or less openly at Yokahama and Hong-
Kong, and the drawings — losers and winners both agree
here — are above reproach.

We have resigned ourselves to the infinite monotony
of a twenty days' voyage. The Pacific Mail advertises
falsely. Only under the most favorable circumstances
of wind and steam can their under-engined boats cover
the distance in fifteen days. Our *City of Peking*, for
instance, had been jogging along at a gentle ten knots
an hour, a pace out of all proportion to her bulk.
"When we get a wind," says the Captain, "we shall
do better." She is a four-master and can carry any
amount of canvas. It is not safe to run steamers
across this void under the poles of Atlantic liners.
The monotony of the sea is paralysing. We have
passed the wreck of a little sealing-schooner lying
bottom up and covered with gulls. She weltered by
in the chill dawn, unlovely as the corpse of a man

and the wild birds piped thinly at us as they steered
her across the surges. The pulse of the Pacific is no
little thing even in the quieter moods of the sea. It
set our bows swinging and nosing and ducking ere
we were a day clear of Yokohama, and yet there was
never swell nor crested wave in sight. "We ride very
high," said the Captain, "and she's a dry boat. She
has a knack of crawling over things somehow; but we
shan't need to put her to the test this journey."

* * * * * * *

The Captain was mistaken. For four days we have
endured the sullen displeasure of the North Pacific,
winding up with a night of discomfort. It began
with a grey sea, flying clouds, and a head-wind that
smote fifty knots off the day's run. Then rose from
the southeast a beam sea warranted by no wind that
was abroad upon the waters in our neighbourhood, and
we wallowed in the trough of it for sixteen mortal
hours. In the stillness of the harbour, when the newspaper man is lunching in her saloon and the steam
launch is crawling round her sides, a ship of pride is a
"stately liner." Out in the open, one rugged shoulder
of a sea between you and the horizon, she becomes "the
old hooker," a "lively boat," and other things of small
import, for this is necessary to propitiate the Ocean.
"There's a storm to the southeast of us," explained the
Captain. "That's what's kicking up this sea."

The *City of Peking* did not belie her reputation. She
crawled over the seas in liveliest wise, never shipping
a bucket till—she was forced to. Then she took it
green over the bows to the vast edification of, at least,

one passenger who had never seen the scuppers full before.

Later in the day the fun began. "Oh, she's a daisy at rolling," murmured the chief steward, flung starfish-wise on a table among his glassware. "She's rolling some," said a black apparition new risen from the stoke-hold. "Is she going to roll any more?" demanded the ladies grouped in what ought to have been the ladies' saloon, but, according to American custom, was labelled "Social Hall."

Passed in the twilight the chief officer — a dripping, bearded face. "Shall I mark out the bull-board?" said he, and lurched aft, followed by the tongue of a wave. "She'll roll her guards under to-night," said a man from Louisiana, where their river-steamers do not understand the meaning of bulwarks. We dined to a dashing accompaniment of crockery, the bounds of emancipated beer bottles livelier than their own corks, and the clamour of the ship's gong broken loose and calling to meals on its own account.

After dinner the real rolling began. She did roll "guards under," as the Louisiana man had prophesied. At thirty-minute intervals to the second arrived one big sea, when the electric lamps died down to nothing, and the screw raved and the blows of the sea made the decks quiver. On those occasions we moved from our chairs, not gently, but discourteously. At other times we were merely holding on with both hands.

It was then that I studied Fear — Terror bound in black silk and fighting hard with herself. For reasons which will be thoroughly understood, there was a tendency among the passengers to herd together and to address in quiries to every officer who happened to stagger through the saloon. No one was in the least alarmed, — oh dear, no! — but all were keenly anxious for information. This anxiety redoubled after a more than usually vicious roll. Terror was a large, handsome, and cultured lady who knew the precise value of human life, the inwardness of *Robert Elsmere*, the latest poetry — everything in fact that a clever woman should know. When the rolling was near its worst, she began to talk swiftly. I do not for a moment believe that she knew what she was talking about. The rolling increased. She buckled down to the task of making conversation. By the heave of the labouring bust, the restless working of the fingers on the tablecloth, and the uncontrollable eyes that turned always to the companion stairhead, I was able to judge the extremity of her fear. Yet her words were frivolous and commonplace enough; they poured forth unceasingly, punctuated with little laughs and giggles, as a woman's speech should be. Presently, a member of her group suggested going to bed. No, she wanted to sit up; she wanted to go on talking, and as long as she could get a soul to sit with her she had her desire. When for sheer lack of company she was forced to get to her cabin, she left reluctantly, looking back to the well-lighted saloon over her shoulder. The contrast between the flowing triviality of her speech and the strained intentness of eye and hand was a quaint thing to behold. I know now how Fear should be painted.

No one slept very heavily that night. Both arms were needed to grip the berth, while the trunks below wound the carpet-slips into knots and battered the fram ing of the cabins.   Once it seemed to me that the whole of the labouring fabric that cased our trumpery fortunes stood on end and in this undignified posture hopped a mighty hop.   Twice I know I shot out of my berth to join the adventurous trunks on the floor.   A hundred times the crash of the wave on the ship's side was followed by the roar of the water, as it swept the decks and raved round the deckhouses.   In a lull I heard the flying feet of a man, a shout, and a far-away chorus of lost spirits singing somebody's requiem.

May 24 (Queen's Birthday). — If ever you meet an American, be good to him.   This day the ship was dressed with flags from stem to stern, and chiefest of the bunting was the Union-Jack.   They had given no word of warning to the English, who were proportionately pleased.   At dinner up rose an ex-Commissioner of the Lucknow Division (on my honour, Anglo-India extends to the ends of the earth!) and gave us the health of Her Majesty and the President.   It was afterwards that the trouble began.   A small American penned half a dozen English into a corner and lectured them soundly on — their want of patriotism!

"What sort of Queen's Birthday do you call this?" he thundered.   "What did you drink our President's health for?   What's the President to you on this day of all others?   Well, suppose you *are* in the minority, all the more reason for standing by your country.   Don't talk to me.   You Britishers made a mess of it — a mighty bungle of the whole thing.   I'm an American of the Americans; but if no one can propose Her Majesty's health better than by just throwing it at your heads, I'm going to try."

Then and there he delivered a remarkably neat little oration — pat, well put together, and clearly delivered. So it came to pass that the Queen's health was best honoured by an American. We English were dazed. I wondered how many Englishmen not trained to addressing their fellows would have spoken half so fluently as the gentleman from 'Frisco.

"Well, you see," said one of us feebly, "she's our Queen, anyhow, and — and — she's been ours for fifty years, and not one of us here has seen England for seven years, and we can't enthuse over the matter. We've lived to be hauled over the coals for want of patriotism by an American! We'll be more careful next time."

And the conversation drifted naturally into the question of the government of men — English, Japanese (we have several travelled Japanese aboard), and Americans throwing the ball from one to another. We bore in mind the golden rule: "Never agree with a man who abuses his own country," and got on well enough.

"Japan," said a little gentleman who was a rich man there, "Japan is divided into two administrative sides. On the one the remains of a very strict and quite Oriental despotism; on the other a mass of — what do you call it? — red-tapeism which is not understood even by the officials who handle it. We copy the red tape, and when it is copied we believe that we administer. That is a vice of all Oriental nations. We are Orientals."

"Oh no, say the most westerly of the westerns," purred an American, soothingly.

The little man was pleased. "Thanks. That is what we hope to believe, but up to the present it is not so

Look now.   A farmer in my country holds a hillside cut
into little terraces.   Every year he must submit to his
Government a statement of the size and revenue paid,
not on the whole hillside, but on each terrace.   The complete statement makes a pile three inches high, and is of
no use when it is made except to keep in work thousands
of officials to check the returns.   Is that administration?
By God! we call it so, but we multiply officials by the
twenty, and *they* are not administration.   What country
is such a fool?   Look at our Government offices eaten
up with clerks!   Some day, I tell you, there will be a
smash."

This was new to me, but I might have guessed it.   In
every country where swords and uniforms accompany
civil office there is a natural tendency towards an ill-
considered increase of officialdom.

"You might pay India a visit some day," I said.   "I
fancy that you would find that our country shares your
trouble."

Thereupon a Japanese gentleman in the Educational
Department began to cross-question me on the matters of
his craft in India, and in a quarter of an hour got from
me the very little that I knew about primary schools,
higher education, and the value of an M. A. degree.   He
knew exactly what he wanted to ask, and only dropped
me when the tooth of Desire had clean picked the bone
of Ignorance.

Then an American held forth, harping on a string that
has already been too often twanged in my ear.   "What
will it be in America itself?"

"The whole system is rotten from top to bottom." he
said.   "As rotten as rotten can be."

"That's so," said the Louisiana man, with an affirmative puff of smoke.

"They call us a Republic. We may be. I don't think it. You Britishers have got the only republic worth the name. You choose to run your ship of state with a gilt figurehead; but I know, and so does every man who has thought about it, that your Queen doesn't cost you one-half what our system of pure democracy costs us. Politics in America? There aren't any. The whole question of the day is spoils. That's all. We fight our souls out over tram-contracts, gas-contracts, road-contracts, and any darned thing that will turn a dishonest dollar, and we call that politics. No one but a low-down man will run for Congress and the Senate — the Senate of the freest people on earth are bound slaves to some blessed monopoly. If I had money enough, I could buy the Senate of the United States, the Eagle, and the Star-Spangled Banner complete."

"And the Irish vote included?" said some one — a Britisher, I fancy.

"Certainly, if I chose to go yahooing down the street at the tail of the British lion. Anything dirty will buy the Irish vote. That's why our politics are dirty. Some day you Britishers will grant Home Rule to the vermin in our blankets. Then the real Americans will invite the Irish to get up and git to where they came from. 'Wish you'd hurry up that time before we have another trouble. We're bound hand and foot by the Irish vote; or at least that's the excuse for any unusual theft that we perpetrate. I tell you there's no good in an Irishman except as a fighter. He doesn't understand work. He has a natural gift of the gab, and he can drink a man blind. These three qualifications make him a first-class politician."

With one accord the Americans present commenced to abuse Ireland and its people as they had met them, and each man prefaced his commination service with: "I am an American by birth — an American from way back."

It must be an awful thing to live in a country where you have to explain that you really belong there. Louder grew the clamour and crisper the sentiments.

"If we weren't among Americans, I should say we were consorting with Russians," said a fellow-countryman in my ear.

"They can't mean what they say," I whispered. "Listen to this fellow." He was saying:

"And I know, for I have been three times round the world and resided in most countries on the Continent, that there was never people yet could govern themselves."

"Allah! This from an American!"

"And who should know better than an American?" was the retort. "For the ignorant — that is to say for the majority — there is only one argument — fear; the fear of Death. In our case we give any scallawag who comes across the water all the same privileges that we have made for ourselves. There we make a mistake. They thank us by playing the fool. Then we shoot them down. You can't persuade the mob of any country to become decent citizens. If they misbehave themselves, shoot them. I saw the bombs thrown at Chicago when our police were blown to bits. I saw the banners in the procession that threw the bombs. All the mottoes on

them were in German. The men were aliens in our
midst, and they were shot down like dogs. I've been in
labour riots and seen the militia go through a crowd
like a finger through tissue paper."

"I was in the riots at New Orleans," said the man
from Louisiana. "We turned the Gatling on the other
crowd, and they were sick."

"Whew! I wonder what would have happened if a
Gatling had been used when the West End riots were in
full swing?" said an Englishman. "If a single rioter
were killed in an English town by the police, the chances
are that the policeman would have to stand his trial for
murder and the Ministry of the day would go out."

"Then you've got all your troubles before you. The
more power you give the people, the more trouble they
will give. With us our better classes are corrupt and
our lower classes are lawless. There are millions of use-
ful, law-abiding citizens, and they are very sick of this
thing. We execute our justice in the streets. The law
courts are no use. Take the case of the Chicago Anarchists. It was all we could do to get 'em hanged;
whereas the dead in the streets had been punished off-
hand. We were sure of *them*. Guess that's the reason
we are so quick to fire on a mob. But it's unfair, all the
same. We receive all these cattle — Anarchists, Social-
ists, and ruffians of every sort — and then we shoot them.
The States are as republican as they make 'em. We
have no use for a man who wants to try any more exper-
iments on the Constitution. We are the biggest people
on God's earth. All the world knows that. We've been
shouting that we are also the greatest people. No one
cares to contradict us but ourselves; and we are now

wondering whether we are what we claim to be. Never mind; you Britishers will have the same experiences to go through. You're beginning to rot now. Your County Councils will make you more rotten because you are putting power into the hands of untrained people. When you reach our level, — every man with a vote and the right to sell it; the right to nominate fellows of his own kidney to swamp out better men, — you'll be what we are now — rotten, rotten, rotten!"

The voice ceased, and no man rose up to contradict.

"We'll worry through it somehow," said the man from Louisiana. "What would do us a world of good now would be a big European war. We're getting slack and sprawly. Now a war outside our borders would make us all pull together. But that's a luxury we shan't get."

"Can't you raise one within your own borders?" I said flippantly, to get rid of the thought of the great blind nation in her unrest putting out her hand to the Sword. Mine was a most unfortunate remark.

"I hope not," said an American, very seriously. "We have paid a good deal to keep ourselves together before this, and it is not likely that we shall split up without protest. Yet some say we are too large, and some say that Washington and the Eastern States are running the whole country. If ever we do divide, — God help us when we do, — it will be East and West this time."

"We built the old hooker too long in the run. We put the engine room aft. Break her back," said an American who had not yet spoken. "'Wonder if our forbears knew how she was going to grow."

"A very large country." The speaker sighed as though the weight of it from New York to 'Frisco lay

upon his shoulders. " If ever we do divide, it means
that we are done for. There is no room for four first-
class empires in the States. One split will lead to
another if the first is successful. What's the use of
talking ? "

What was the use? Here's our conversation as it
ran, the night of the Queen's Birthday. What do *you*
think ?

No. XXIII

> "Serene, indifferent to fate,
> Thou sittest at the western gate,
> Thou seest the white seas fold their tents,
> Oh warder of two Continents.
> Thou drawest all things small and great
> To thee beside the Western Gate."

THIS is what Bret Harte has written of the great city
of San Francisco, and for the past fortnight I have been
wondering what made him do it. There is neither seren-
ity nor indifference to be found in these parts; and evil
would it be for the Continent whose wardship were in-
trusted to so reckless a guardian. Behold me pitched
neck-and-crop from twenty days of the High Seas, into
the whirl of California, deprived of any guidance, and
left to draw my own conclusions. Protect me from
the wrath of an outraged community if these letters be
ever read by American eyes. San Francisco is a mad
city — inhabited for the most part by perfectly insane
people whose women are of a remarkable beauty. When
the *City of Peking* steamed through the Golden Gate I saw
with great joy that the block-house which guarded the
mouth of the " finest harbour in the the world, Sir," could
be silenced by two gunboats from Hong-Kong with safety,
comfort, and despatch.

Then a reporter leaped aboard, and ere I could gasp held me in his toils. He pumped me exhaustively while I was getting ashore, demanding, of all things in the world, news about Indian journalism. It is an awful thing to enter a new land with a new lie on your lips. I spoke the truth to the evil-minded Custom-house man who turned my most sacred raiment on a floor composed of stable-refuse and pine-splinters; but the reporter overwhelmed me not so much by his poignant audacity as his beautiful ignorance. I am sorry now that I did not tell him more lies as I passed into a city of three hundred thousand white men. Think of it! Three hundred thousand white men and women gathered in one spot, walking upon real pavements in front of real plate-glass windowed shops, and talking something that was not very different from English. It was only when I had tangled myself up in a hopeless maze of small wooden houses, dust, street-refuse, and children who play with empty kerosene tins, that I discovered the difference of speech.

"You want to go to the Palace Hotel?" said an affable youth on a dray. "What in hell are you doing here, then? This is about the lowest place in the city. Go six blocks north to corner of Geary and Market; then walk around till you strike corner of Gutter and Sixteenth, and that brings you there."

I do not vouch for the literal accuracy of these directions, quoting but from a disordered memory.

"Amen," I said. "But who am I that I should strike the corners of such as you name? Peradventure they be gentlemen of repute, and might hit back. Bring it down to dots, my son."

I thought he would have smitten me, but he didn't.

He explained that no one ever used the word "street," and that every one was supposed to know how the streets run; for sometimes the names were upon the lamps and sometimes they weren't. Fortified with these directions I proceeded till I found a mighty street full of sumptuous buildings four or five stories high, but paved with rude cobble stones in the fashion of the Year One. A cable-car without any visible means of support slid stealthily behind me and nearly struck me in the back. A hundred yards further there was a slight commotion in the street — a gathering together of three or four — and something that glittered as it moved very swiftly. A ponderous Irish gentleman with priest's cords in his hat and a small nickel-plated badge on his fat bosom emerged from the knot, supporting a Chinaman who had been stabbed in the eye and was bleeding like a pig. The bystanders went their ways, and the Chinaman, assisted by the policeman, his own. Of course this was none of my business, but I rather wanted to know what had happened to the gentleman who had dealt the stab. It said a great deal for the excellence of the municipal arrangements of the town that a surging crowd did not at once block the street to see what was going forward. I was the sixth man and the last who assisted at the performance, and my curiosity was six times the greatest. Indeed, I felt ashamed of showing it.

There were no more incidents till I reached the Palace Hotel, a seven-storied warren of humanity with a thousand rooms in it. All the travel-books will tell you about hotel arrangements in this country. They should be seen to be appreciated. Understand clearly — and this letter is written after a thousand miles of experiances — that money will not buy you service in the West.

When the hotel clerk — the man who awards your room to you and who is supposed to give you information — when that resplendent individual stoops to attend to your wants, he does so whistling or humming, or picking his teeth, or pauses to converse with some one he knows. These performances, I gather, are to impress upon you that he is a free man and your equal. From his general appearance and the size of his diamonds he ought to be your superior. There is no necessity for this swaggering, self-consciousness of freedom. Business is business, and the man who is paid to attend to a man might reasonably devote his whole attention to the job.

In a vast marble-paved hall under the glare of an electric light sat forty or fifty men; and for their use and amusement were provided spittoons of infinite capacity and generous gape. Most of the men wore frock-coats and top-hats, — the things that we in India put on at a wedding breakfast if we possessed them, — but they all spat. They spat on principle. The spittoons were on the staircases, in each bedroom — yea, and in chambers even more sacred than these. They chased one into retirement, but they blossomed in chiefest splendour round the Bar, and they were all used, every reeking one of 'em. Just before I began to feel deathly sick, another reporter grappled me. What he wanted to know was the precise area of India in square miles. I referred him to Whittaker. He had never heard of Whittaker. He wanted it from my own mouth, and I would not tell him. Then he swerved off, like the other man, to details of journalism in our own country. I ventured

to suggest that the interior economy of a paper most con
cerned the people who worked it. "That's the very
thing that interests us," he said. "Have you got re
porters anything like our reporters on Indian news
papers?" "We have not," I said, and suppressed the
"thank God" rising to my lips. "*Why* haven't you?"
said he. "Because they would die," I said. It was ex·
actly like talking to a child — a very rude little child.
He would begin almost every sentence with: "Now tell
me something about India," and would turn aimlessly
from one question to another without the least conti·
nuity. I was not angry, but keenly interested. The man
was a revelation to me. To his questions I returned
answers mendacious and evasive. After all, it really did
not matter what I said. He could not understand. I
can only hope and pray that none of the readers of the
Pioneer will ever see that portentous interview. The
man made me out to be an idiot several sizes more
drivelling than my destiny intended, and the rankness
of his ignorance managed to distort the few poor facts
with which I supplied him into large and elaborate lies.
Then thought I: "The matter of American journalism
shall be looked into later on. At present I will enjoy
myself."

No man rose to tell me what were the lions of the
place. No one volunteered any sort of conveyance. I
was absolutely alone in this big city of white folk. By
instinct I sought refreshment and came upon a bar-room,
full of bad Salon pictures, in which men with hats on
the backs of their heads were wolfing food from a counter.
It was the institution of the "Free Lunch" that I had
struck. You paid for a drink and got as much as you

wanted to eat. For something less than a rupee a day a man can feed himself sumptuously in San Francisco, even though he be bankrupt. Remember this if ever you are stranded in these parts.

Later, I began a vast but unsystematic exploration of the streets. I asked for no names. It was enough that the pavements were full of white men and women, the streets clanging with traffic, and that the restful roar of a great city rang in my ears. The cable-cars glided to all points of the compass. I took them one by one till I could go no farther. San Francisco has been pitched down on the sand-bunkers of the Bikaneer desert. About one-fourth of it is ground reclaimed from the sea — any old-timer will tell you all about that. The remainder is ragged, unthrifty sand-hills, pegged down by houses.

From an English point of view there has not been the least attempt at grading those hills, and indeed you might as well try to grade the hillocks of Sind. The cable-cars have for all practical purposes made San Francisco a dead level. They take no count of rise or fall, but slide equably on their appointed courses from one end to the other of a six-mile street. They turn corners almost at right angles; cross other lines, and, for aught I know, may run up the sides of houses. There is no visible agency of their flight; but once in a while you shall pass a five-storied building, humming with machinery that winds up an everlasting wire-cable, and the initiated will tell you that here is the mechanism. I gave up asking questions. If it pleases Providence to make a car run up and down a slit in the ground for many miles, and if for twopence-halfpenny I can ride in that car, why shall I seek the reasons of the miracle?

Rather let me look out of the windows till the shops
give place to thousands and thousands of little houses
made of wood — each house just big enough for a man
and his family. Let me watch the people in the cars,
and try to find out in what manner they differ from
us, their ancestors. They delude themselves into the
belief that they talk English, — *the* English, — and I
have already been pitied for speaking with "an English accent." The man who pitied me spoke, so far
as I was concerned, the language of thieves. And
they all do. Where we put the accent forward, they
throw it back, and *vice versa;* where we use the long *a,*
they use the short; and words so simple as to be past
mistaking, they pronounce somewhere up in the dome
of their heads. How do these things happen? Oliver
Wendell Holmes says that Yankee schoolmarms, the
cider, and the salt codfish of the Eastern States are
responsible for what he calls a nasal accent. A Hindu
is a Hindu, and a brother to the man who knows his
vernacular; and a Frenchman is French because he
speaks his own language; but the American has no
language. He is dialect, slang, provincialism, accent,
and so forth. Now that I have heard their voices, all
the beauty of Bret Harte is being ruined for me, because
I find myself catching through the roll of his rhythmi-
cal prose the cadence of his peculiar fatherland. Get an
American lady to read to you "How Santa Claus came to
Simpson's Bar," and see how much is, under her tongue,
left of the beauty of the original.

But I am sorry for Bret Harte. It happened this way.
A reporter asked me what I thought of the city, and I
made answer suavely that it was hallowed ground to me

because of Bret Harte. That was true. "Well," said the reporter, "Bret Harte claims California, but California don't claim Bret Harte. He's been so long in England that he's quite English. Have you seen our cracker-factories and the new offices of the *Examiner* ?" He could not understand that to the outside world the city was worth a great deal less than the man.

* * * * * * *

Night fell over the Pacific, and the white sea-fog whipped through the streets, dimming the splendours of the electric lights. It is the use of this city, her men and women, to parade between the hours of eight and ten a certain street, called Kearney Street, where the finest shops are situated. Here the click of heels on the pavement is loudest, here the lights are brightest, and here the thunder of the traffic is most overwhelming. I watched Young California and saw that it was at least expensively dressed, cheerful in manner, and self-asserting in conversation. Also the women are very fair. The maidens were of generous build, large, well-groomed, and attired in raiment that even to my inexperienced eyes must have cost much. Kearney Street, at nine o'clock, levels all distinctions of rank as impartially as the grave. Again and again I loitered at the heels of a couple of resplendent beings, only to overhear, when I expected the level voice of culture, the *staccato* "Sez he," "Sez I," that is the mark of the white servant-girl all the world over.

This was depressing because, in spite of all that goes to the contrary, fine feathers ought to make fine birds. There was wealth — unlimited wealth — in the streets,

but not an accent that would not have been dear at fifty
cents. Wherefore, revolving in my mind that these folk
were barbarians, I was presently enlightened and made
aware that they also were the heirs of all the ages, and
civilised after all. There appeared before me an affable
stranger of prepossessing appearance, with a blue and an
innocent eye. Addressing me by name, he claimed to
have met me in New York at the Windsor, and to this
claim I gave a qualified assent. I did not remember the
fact, but since he was so certain of it, why then — I
waited developments. "And what did you think of
Indiana when you came through?" was the next question. It revealed the mystery of previous acquaintance,
and one or two other things. With reprehensible carelessness, my friend of the light-blue eye had looked up
the name of his victim in the hotel register and read
"India" for Indiana. He could not imagine an Englishman coming through the States from West to East
instead of by the regularly ordained route. My fear
was that in his delight at finding me so responsive
he would make remarks about New York and the
Windsor which I could not understand. And indeed,
he adventured in this direction once or twice, asking
me what I thought of such and such streets, which,
from his tone, I gathered were anything but respectable.
It is trying to talk unknown New York in almost unknown San Francisco. But my friend was merciful.
He protested that I was one after his own heart, and
pressed upon me rare and curious drinks at more than
one bar. These drinks I accepted with gratitude, as
also the cigars with which his pockets were stored. He
would show me the Life of the city. Having no desire

to watch a weary old play again, I evaded the offer, and received in lieu of the Devil's instruction much coarse flattery. Curiously constituted is the soul of man. Knowing how and where this man lied, waiting idly for the finale, I was distinctly conscious, as he bubbled compliments in my ear, of soft thrills of gratified pride. I was wise, quoth he, anybody could see that with half an eye; sagacious; versed in the affairs of the world; an acquaintance to be desired; one who had tasted the cup of Life with discretion. All this pleased me, and in a measure numbed the suspicion that was thoroughly aroused. Eventually the blue-eyed one discovered, nay insisted, that I had a taste for cards (this was clumsily worked in, but it was my fault, in that I met him half-way, and allowed him no chance of good acting). Hereupon, I laid my head to one side, and simulated unholy wisdom, quoting odds and ends of poker-talk, all ludicrously misapplied. My friend kept his countenance admirably; and well he might, for five minutes later we arrived, always by the purest of chances, at a place where we could play cards, and also frivol with Louisiana State Lottery tickets. Would I play? "Nay," said I, "for to me cards have neither meaning nor continuity; but let us assume that I am going to play. How would you and your friends get to work? Would you play a straight game, or make me drunk, or — well, the fact is I'm a newspaper man, and I'd be much obliged if you'd let me know something about bunco-steering." My blue-eyed friend cursed me by his gods, — the Right and the Left Bower; he even cursed the very good cigars he had given me. But, the storm over, he quieted down and explained. I

apologised for causing him to waste an evening, and
we spent a very pleasant time together. Inaccuracy,
provincialism, and a too hasty rushing to conclusions
were the rocks that he had split on; but he got his re-
venge when he said: "How would I play with you? From
all the poppycock" (*Anglice*, bosh) "you talked about
poker, I'd ha' played a straight game and skinned you.
I wouldn't have taken the trouble to make you drunk.
You never knew anything of the game; but the way
I was mistaken in you makes me sick." He glared at
me as though I had done him an injury. To-day I
know how it is that, year after year, week after week,
the bunco-steerer, who is the confidence-trick and the
card-sharper man of other climes, secures his prey. He
slavers them over with flattery, as the snake slavers the
rabbit. The incident depressed me because it showed I
had left the innocent East far behind, and was come to
a country where a man must look out for himself. The
very hotel bristled with notices about keeping my door
locked, and depositing my valuables in a safe. The white
man in a lump is bad. Weeping softly for O-Toyo (little
I knew then that my heart was to be torn afresh from my
bosom!), I fell asleep in the clanging hotel.

Next morning I had entered upon the Deferred In
heritance. There are no princes in America, — at least
with crowns on their heads, — but a generous-minded
member of some royal family received my letter of
introduction. Ere the day closed I was a member of the
two clubs and booked for many engagements to dinner
and party. Now this prince, upon whose financial operations be continual increase, had no reason, nor had the
others, his friends, to put himself out for the sake of one

Briton more or less; but he rested not till he had accomplished all in my behalf that a mother could think of for her *débutante* daughter. Do you know the Bohemian Club of San Francisco? They say its fame extends over the world. It was created somewhat on the lines of the Savage by men who wrote or drew things, and it has blossomed into most unrepublican luxury. The ruler of the place is an owl — an owl standing upon a skull and cross-bones, showing forth grimly the wisdom of the man of letters and the end of his hopes for immortality. The owl stands on the staircase, a statue four feet high, is carved in the woodwork, flutters on the frescoed ceilings, is stamped on the note paper, and hangs on the walls. He is an Ancient and Honourable Bird. Under his wing 'twas my privilege to meet with white men whose lives were not chained down to routine of toil, who wrote magazine articles instead of reading them hurriedly in the pauses of office-work, who painted pictures instead of contenting themselves with cheap etchings picked up at another man's sale of effects. Mine were all the rights of social intercourse that India, stony-hearted step-mother of Collectors, has swindled us out of. Treading soft carpets and breathing the incense of superior cigars, I wandered from room to room studying the paintings in which the members of the club had caricatured themselves, their associates, and their aims. There was a slick French audacity about the workmanship of these men of toil unbending that went straight to the heart of the beholder. And yet it was not altogether French. A dry grimness of treatment, almost Dutch, marked the difference. The men painted as they spoke — with certainty. The club indulges in revelries which it calls "jinks"—high and low,—at intervals,—and each of these gatherings is faithfully portrayed in oils by hands that know their business. In this club were no amateurs spoiling canvas because they fancied they could handle oils without knowledge of shadows or anatomy—no gentleman of leisure ruining the temper of publishers and an already ruined market with atttempts to write "because everybody writes something these days." My hosts were working, or had worked, for their daily bread with pen or paint, and their talk for the most part was of the shop shoppy—that is to say, delightful. They extended a large hand of welcome and were as brethren, and I did homage to the Owl and listened to their talk. An Indian Club about Christmas-time will yield, if properly worked, an abundant harvest of queer tales; but at a gathering of Americans from the uttermost ends of their own continent the tales are larger, thicker, more spinous, and even more azure than any Indian variety. Tales of the War I heard told by an ex-officer of the South over his evening drink to a Colonel of the Northern army; my introducer, who had served as a trooper in the Northern Horse, throwing in emendations from time to time.

Other voices followed with equally wondrous tales of riata-throwing in Mexico or Arizona, of gambling at army posts in Texas, of newspaper wars waged in godless Chicago, of deaths sudden and violent in Montana and Dakota, of the loves of half-breed maidens in the South, and fantastic huntings for gold in mysterious Alaska. Above all, they told the story of the building of old San Francisco, when the "finest collection of humanity on God's earth, Sir, started this town, and the water

came up to the foot of Market Street." Very terrible
were some of the tales, grimly humorous the others, and
the men in broadcloth and fine linen who told them had
played their parts in them.

"And now and again when things got too bad they
would toll the city bell, and the Vigilance Committee
turned out and hanged the suspicious characters. A man
didn't begin to be suspected in those days till he had
committed at least one unprovoked murder," said a calm-
eyed, portly old gentleman. I looked at the pictures
around me, the noiseless, neat-uniformed waiter behind
me, the oak-ribbed ceiling above, the velvety carpet beneath. It was hard to realise that even twenty years ago
you could see a man hanged with great pomp. Later on
I found reason to change my opinion. The tales gave
me a headache and set me thinking. How in the world
was it possible to take in even one-thousandth of this
huge, roaring, many-sided continent? In the silence of
the sumptuous library lay Professor Bryce's book on
the American Republic. "It is an omen," said I. "He
has done all things in all seriousness, and he may be purchased for half a guinea. Those who desire information
of the most undoubted must refer to his pages. For
me is the daily round of vagabondage, the recording of
the incidents of the hour, and talk with the travelling
companion of the day. I will not 'do' this country at
all."

And I forgot all about India for ten days while I went
out to dinners and watched the social customs of the
people, which are entirely different from our customs,
and was introduced to the men of many millions. These
persons are harmless in their earlier stages; that is to

G

say, a man worth three or four million dollars may be a good talker, clever, amusing, and of the world; a man with twice that amount is to be avoided; and a twenty-million man is — just twenty millions. Take an instance. I was speaking to a newspaper man about seeing the proprietor of his journal. My friend snorted indignantly: "See *him!* Great Scott! *No!* If he happens to appear in the office, I have to associate with him; but, thank Heaven, outside of that I move in circles where he cannot come."

And yet the first thing I have been taught to believe is that money was everything in America!

SHOWS HOW THROUGH FOLLY I ASSISTED AT A MURDER
AND WAS AFRAID.   THE RULE OF THE DEMOCRACY
AND THE DESPOTISM OF THE ALIEN.

"Poor men — God made, and all for that!"

IT was a bad business throughout, and the only consolation is that it was all my fault.   A man took me round
the Chinese quarter of San Francisco, which is a ward
of the city of Canton set down in the most eligible
business-quarter of the place.   The Chinaman with his
usual skill has possessed himself of good brick fire-proof
buildings and, following instinct, has packed each tenement with hundreds of souls, all living in filth and
squalor not to be appreciated save by you in India.
That cursory investigation ought to have sufficed; but
I wanted to know how deep in the earth the Pig-tail had
taken root.   Therefore I explored the Chinese quarter
a second time and alone, which was foolishness.   No one
in the filthy streets (but for the blessed sea breezes San
Francisco would enjoy cholera every season) interfered
with my movements, though many asked for *cumshaw*.
I struck a house about four stories high full of celestial
abominations, and began to burrow down; having heard
that these tenements were constructed on the lines of
icebergs — two-thirds below sight level.   Downstairs I

crawled past Chinamen in bunks, opium-smokers, brothels, and gambling hells, till I had reached the second cellar — was in fact, in the labyrinths of a warren. Great is the wisdom of the Chinaman. In time of trouble that house could be razed to the ground by the mob, and yet hide all its inhabitants in brick-walled and wooden-beamed subterranean galleries, strengthened with iron-framed doors and gates. On the second underground floor a man asked for *cumshaw* and took me downstairs to yet another cellar, where the air was as thick as butter, and the lamps burned little holes in it not more than an inch square. In this place a poker club had assembled and was in full swing. The Chinaman loves "pokel," and plays it with great skill, swearing like a cat when he loses. Most of the men round the table were in semi-European dress, their pig-tails curled up under billy-cock hats. One of the company looked like a Eurasian, whence I argued that he was a Mexican — a supposition that later inquiries confirmed. They were a picturesque set of fiends and polite, being too absorbed in their game to look at the stranger. We were all deep down under the earth, and save for the rustle of a blue gown sleeve and the ghostly whisper of the cards as they were shuffled and played, there was no sound. The heat was almost unendurable. There was some dispute between the Mexican and the man on his left. The latter shifted his place to put the table between himself and his opponent, and stretched a lean yellow hand towards the Mexican's winnings.

Mark how purely man is a creature of instinct. Rarely introduced to the pistol, I saw the Mexican half rise in his chair and at the same instant found myself full length on the floor. None had told me that this was the best attitude when bullets are abroad. I was there prone before I had time to think — dropping as the room was filled with an intolerable clamour like the discharge of a cannon. In those close quarters the pistol report had no room to spread any more than the smoke — then acrid in my nostrils. There was no second shot, but a great silence in which I rose slowly to my knees. The China-man was gripping the table with both hands and staring in front of him at an empty chair. The Mexican had gone, and a little whirl of smoke was floating near the roof. Still gripping the table, the Chinaman said: "Ah!" in the tone that a man would use when, looking up from his work suddenly, he sees a well-known friend in the doorway. Then he coughed and fell over to his own right, and I saw that he had been shot in the stomach.

I became aware that, save for two men leaning over the stricken one, the room was empty; and all the tides of intense fear, hitherto held back by intenser curiosity, swept over my soul. I ardently desired the outside air. It was possible that the Chinamen would mistake me for the Mexican, — everything horrible seemed possible just then, — and it was more than possible that the stairways would be closed while they were hunting for the mur-derer. The man on the floor coughed a sickening cough. I heard it as I fled, and one of his companions turned out the lamp. Those stairs seemed interminable, and to add to my dismay there was no sound of commotion in the house. No one hindered, no one even looked at me. There was no trace of the Mexican. I found the doorway and, my legs trembling under me, reached the protection of the clear cool night, the fog, and the rain. I dared not run, and for the life of me I could not walk. I must have effected a compromise, for I remember the light of a street lamp showed the shadow of one half skipping — caracoling along the pavements in what seemed to be an ecstacy of suppressed happiness. But it was fear — deadly fear. Fear compounded of past knowledge of the Oriental — only other white man — available witness — three stories underground — and the cough of the Chinaman now some forty feet under my clattering boot-heels. It was good to see the shop-fronts and electric lights again. Not for anything would I have informed the police, because I firmly believed that the Mexican had been dealt with somewhere down there on the third floor long ere I had reached the air; and, moreover, once clear of the place, I could not for the life of me tell where it was. My ill-considered flight brought me out somewhere a mile distant from the hotel; and the clank of the lift that bore me to a bed six stories above ground was music in my ears. Wherefore I would impress it upon you who follow after, do not knock about the Chinese quarters at night and alone. You may stumble across a picturesque piece of human nature that will unsteady your nerves for half a day.

*   *   *   *   *   *   *

And this brings me by natural sequence to the great drink question. As you know, of course, the American does not drink at meals as a sensible man should. Indeed, he has no meals. He stuffs for ten minutes thrice a day. Also he has no decent notions about the sun being over the yard-arm or below the horizon. He pours his vanity into himself at unholy hours, and indeed he can hardly help it. You have no notion of what "treating" means on the Western slope. It is more than an institution; it is a religion, though men tell me that it is nothing to what it was. Take a very common instance. At 10.30 A.M. a man is smitten with desire for stimulants. He is in the company of two friends. All three adjourn to the nearest bar, — seldom more than twenty yards away, — and take three straight whiskys. They talk for two minutes. The second and third man then treats in order; and thus each walks into the street, two of them the poorer by three goes of whisky under their belt and one with two more liquors than he wanted. It is not etiquette yet to refuse a treat. The result is peculiar. I have never yet, I confess, seen a drunken man in the streets, but I have heard more about drunkenness among white men, and seen more decent men above or below themselves with drink, than I care to think about. And the vice runs up into all sorts of circles and societies. Never was I more astonished than at one pleasant dinner party to hear a pair of pretty lips say casually of a gentleman friend then under discussion, "He was drunk." The fact was merely stated without emotion. That was what startled me. But the climate of California deals kindly with excess, and treacherously covers up its traces. A man neither bloats nor shrivels in this dry air. He continues with the false bloom of health upon his cheeks, an equable eye, a firm mouth, and a steady hand till a day of reckoning arrives, and suddenly breaking up, about the head, he dies, and his friends speak his epitaph accordingly. Why people who in most cases cannot hold their liquor should play with it so recklessly I leave to others to decide. This unhappy state of affairs has, however, produced one good result which I will confide to you. In the heart of the business quarter, where banks and bankers are thickest, and telegraph wires most numerous, stands a semi-subterranean bar tended by a German with long blond locks and a crystalline eye. Go thither softly, treading on the tips of your toes, and ask him for a Button Punch. 'Twill take ten minutes to brew, but the result is the highest and noblest product of the age. No man but one knows what is in it. I have a theory it is compounded of the shavings of cherubs' wings, the glory of a tropical dawn, the red clouds of sunset, and fragments of lost epics by dead masters. But try you for yourselves, and pause a while to bless me, who am always mindful of the truest interests of my brethren.

But enough of the stale spilth of bar-rooms. Turn now to the august spectacle of a Government of the people, by the people, for the people, as it is understood in the city of San Francisco. Professor Bryce's book will tell you that every American citizen over twenty one years of age possesses a vote. He may not knôw how to run his own business, control his wife, or instil reverence into his children, may be pauper, half-crazed with drink, bankrupt, dissolute, or merely a born fool; but he has a vote. If he likes, he can be voting most of his time — voting for his State Governor, his municipal officers, local option, sewage contracts, or anything else of which he has no special knowledge.

Once every four years he votes for a new President. In his spare moments he votes for his own judges — the men who shall give him justice. These are dependent on popular favour for re-election inasmuch as they are but chosen for a term of years — two or three, I believe. Such a position is manifestly best calculated to create an independent and unprejudiced administrator. Now this mass of persons who vote is divided into two parties — Republican and Democrat. They are both agreed in thinking that the other part is running creation (which is America) into red flame. Also the Democrat as a party drinks more than the Republican, and when drunk may be heard to talk about a thing called the Tariff, which he does not understand, but which he conceives to be the bulwark of the country or else the surest power for its destruction. Sometimes he says one thing and sometimes another, in order to contradict the Republican, who is always contradicting himself. And this is a true and lucid account of the forepart of American politics. The behind-part is otherwise.

Since every man has a vote and may vote on every conceivable thing, it follows that there exist certain wise men who understand the art of buying up votes retail, and vending them wholesale to whoever wants them most urgently. Now an American engaged in making a home for himself has not time to vote for turn-cocks and district attorneys and cattle of that kind, but the unemployed have much time because they are always on hand somewhere in the streets. They are called "the boys," and form a peculiar class. The boys are young men; inexpert in war, unskilled in labour; who have neither killed a man, lifted cattle, or dug a well. In plain English, they are just the men in the streets who can always be trusted to rally round any cause that has a glass of liquor for a visible heart. They wait — they are on hand — ; and in being on hand lies the crown and the glory of American politics. The wise man is he who, keeping a liquor-saloon and judiciously dispensing drinks, knows how to retain within arm's reach a block of men who will vote for or against anything under the canopy of Heaven. Not every saloon-keeper can do this. It demands careful study of city politics, tact, the power of conciliation, and infinite resources of anecdote to amuse and keep the crowd together night after night, till the saloon becomes a salon. Above all, the liquor side of the scheme must not be worked for immediate profit. The boys who drink so freely will ultimately pay their host a thousandfold. An Irishman, and an Irishman pre-eminently, knows how to work such a saloon parliament. Observe for a moment the plan of operations. The rank and file are treated to drink and a little money — and they vote. He who controls ten votes receives a proportionate reward; the dispenser of a thousand votes is worthy of reverence, and so the chain runs on till we reach the most successful worker of public saloons — the man most skilful in keeping his items together and using them when required. Such a man governs the city as absolutely as a king. And you would know where the gain comes in? The whole of the public offices of a city (with the exception of a very few where special technical skill is required) are short-term offices distributed according to "political" leanings. What would you have? A big city requires many officials. Each office carries a salary and influence worth twice the pay. The offices are for the representatives of the men who keep together and are on hand to vote. The Commissioner of Sewage, let us say, is a gentleman who has been elected to his office by a Republican vote. He knows little and cares less about sewage, but he has sense enough to man the pumping-works and the street-sweeping-machines with the gentlemen who elected him. The Commissioner of Police has been helped to his post very largely by the influence of the boys at such and such a saloon. He may be the guardian of city morals, but he is not going to allow his subordinates to enforce early closing or abstention from gambling in that saloon. Most offices are limited to four years, consequently he is a fool who does not make his office pay him while he is in it.

The only people who suffer by this happy arrangement are, in fact, the people who devised the lovely system. And they suffer because they are Americans. Let us explain. As you know, every big city here holds at least one big foreign vote — generally Irish, frequently German. In San Francisco, the gathering place of the races, there is a distinct Italian vote to be considered, but the Irish vote is more important. For this reason the Irishman does not kill himself with overwork. He is made for the cheery dispensing of liquors, for everlasting blarney, and possesses a wonderfully keen appreciation of the weaknesses of lesser human nature. Also he has no sort of conscience, and only one strong conviction — that of deep-rooted hatred toward England. He keeps to the streets, he is on hand, he votes joyously, spending days lavishly, — and time is the American's dearest commodity. Behold the glorious result. To-day the city of San Francisco is governed by the Irish vote and the Irish influence, under the rule of a gentleman whose sight is impaired, and who requires a man to lead him about the streets.

He is called officially "Boss Buckley," and unofficially
the "Blind White Devil." I have before me now the
record of his amiable career in black and white.
It occupies four columns of small print, and perhaps
you would think it disgraceful. Summarised, it is
as follows: Boss Buckley, by tact and deep knowledge
of the seamy side of the city, won himself a following of voters. He sought no office himself, or rarely:
but as his following increased he sold their services to
the highest bidder, himself taking toll of the revenues
of every office. He controlled the Democratic party in
the city of San Francisco. The people appoint their
own judges. Boss Buckley's people appointed judges.
These judges naturally were Boss Buckley's property.
I have been to dinner parties and heard educated men,
not concerned with politics, telling stories one to another
of "justice," both civil and criminal, being bought with
a price from the hands of these judges. Such tales they
told without heat, as men recording facts. Contracts
for road-mending, public buildings, and the like are
under the control of Boss Buckley, because the men
whom Buckley's following sent to the City Council ad-
judicate on these contracts; and on each and every one
of these contracts Boss Buckley levies his percentage for
himself and his allies.

The Republican party in San Francisco also have
their boss. He is not so great a genius as Boss Buckley, but I decline to believe that he is any whit more
virtuous. He has a smaller number of votes at his
command.